Eerie
NEW MEXICO

Eerie
NEW MEXICO

Ray John de Aragón

THE
History
PRESS

Published by The History Press
Charleston, SC
www.historypress.com

Front cover seal illustration by Kari Ann Shultz. *Unless otherwise noted, all images are from the author's collection.*

Opposite: Presentation page.

First published 2020

Manufactured in the United States

ISBN 9781467145947

Library of Congress Control Number: 2020941411

Notice: The information in this book is true and complete to the best of our knowledge. It is offered without guarantee on the part of the author or The History Press. The author and The History Press disclaim all liability in connection with the use of this book.

PRESENTED

TO:

BY:

CONTENTS

DEDICATION AND MEMORIES

This book is dedicated to Fray Francisco Juan de Padilla, New Mexico's Spanish martyr who died around November 30, 1544. His remains, buried at the San Augustine de la Isleta Church at Isleta Pueblo, New Mexico, were discovered to be incorruptible. Religious pilgrims removed relics from the un-decaying body with its perfumed aroma. The faithful revered Fray de Padilla and prayed to him for miracles. A continuing mystery that still persists involved the rising of his coffin. The casket appeared periodically above ground, although it was always buried deep into the earth. In 1895, Father Antonin Jean Baptiste Docher (1852–1928), a French Franciscan Roman Catholic pastor at the church, credited touching the remains and praying to the fray for a miraculous medical cure he personally experienced. Doctors in Albuquerque were totally confounded by the Father Docher's complete and inexplicable recovery from a gangrenous limb that had to be removed to save the priest's life. Docher found the wound that caused the fray's death—while protecting peaceful Jumano Indians, a warring tribe killed him—and he touched the wound. Father Docher investigated ancient claims by the Indians that the fray's spirit would appear at night and travel around the pueblo. King Albert of Belgium and the queen sought the priest out and visited Isleta to learn more about Fray de Padilla. A papal legate, as an official envoy, also reported back to Pope Pius IX. Noted anthropologist Adolph Bandelier was a personal friend of Father Docher, and they both tracked leads into archaeological mysteries in and around Isleta. The Indians called Docher Tashide, which means "little helper" in Tewa. The full story of Fray de Padilla is in my book *Hidden History of Spanish New Mexico*.

A special dedication goes out to Sor María de Jesús de Agreda, who, while serving as the mother superior of a convent in Spain, reportedly appeared through bilocation and ministered among the Jumano and other Indians in New Mexico. The Indians claimed the nun performed various miracles among them and spoke in their native tongues. The Roman Catholic Church has declared Sor Maria "venerable," which leads to sainthood. This Spanish nun has often been proclaimed as New Mexico's saint. Pilgrimages to the sites of her appearances are scheduled annual events.

This book is also dedicated to my mother, María Cleofas Sánchez de Aragón, who was born in 1915 in the village of Peñasco Blanco in northern New Mexico. When I was a little boy, she would tell me strange but appealing stories about beliefs in the supernatural and end them by saying, "Reclame a todos los santos." I called on all of the saints she told me to save me, bless me and protect me. She firmly believed in mysterious powers and things that are unknown or beyond our human comprehension. My mother also had faith that the divine could intercede on our behalf when there were no other rational explanations for things that could do us harm, and the holy spirits would be there for us. Coming from a rural and isolated Spanish colonial village that maintained its ancient roots stemming from the seventeenth century, my mother was able to pass this very rich cultural heritage on to me. What I learned and I personally experienced are between the pages of this unusual book, full of unexplained eerie mysteries of New Mexico.

On February 19, 1955, my first-grade teacher at Lew Wallace Elementary School in Albuquerque, New Mexico, died in a plane crash. Her name was Lois Dean. She was a passenger on TWA Flight 260. Everyone on board died when the airliner hit the cloud-shrouded crest at the Sandia Mountains east of Albuquerque. I was not only stunned but also devastated. Miss Dean always told our class to strive for the stars—especially so when she passed out clay to all of us—and I immediately went to work. She asked what I was doing, and I answered I was making knights. She asked if I knew what that was, and I said yes. Another time she gave us brushes and paint. I painted a large crawling figure and told her it was a lobster. She was surprised by the high level of the work and praised it immensely. We all called her "Miss Green" rather than Dean. She always smiled. I have never forgotten her. This teacher strived to have us use our creative energies and our imagination. Her untimely death touched the entire school. We recounted what she meant to us as her former first graders during a memorial at the school. She lived on in my early dreams, always teaching me.

In fifth grade, Nellie F. Stein challenged us in spectacular ways. She had us doing timelines from ancient history up to World War II. We studied world and U.S. geography and contacted chambers of commerce all over the country. We reported what we learned about capital cities in class, wrote book reports each week and analyzed popular books. Each week, there were spell-offs. We all knew how to write correspondence letters, and we knew about the workings of our national American government. That year, Miss Stein asked what we wanted to be when we grew up. I answered I wanted to be an archaeologist and a writer.

As a university student, I went up with a group on the Tramway to the crest on the Sandia Mountains, to an elevation of 10,678 feet. A guide pointed out the area where the TWA crashed. We could see pieces of the airplane and belongings scattered around although this was many years after the crash, which made national and world news. He also showed us the general region of the Sandia Cave where remnants of prehistoric humans were found, and he talked about this major discovery. After reaching the top, I descended the mountains on a winding foot trail. I searched for old landmarks as I walked down. At the end of the day, I finally reached my car as the moon lit up my path. In memory of all of the teachers who strongly influenced my career as an educator, writer, artist and historian, I dedicate this work to them.

Historical Setting

AN ENCHANTED LAND AND CULTURE

Some years ago, a National Latino Museum showcasing the direct contributions of Hispanics to the history of the United States was proposed. This new museum was to be built in Washington, D.C. A commission to study Latino contributions to the history of the United States was appointed. The committee, which was composed of representatives from the Cuban, Puerto Rican, Dominican and Mexican communities, met at the National Hispanic Cultural Center in Albuquerque. Surprisingly, New Mexico Latinos were left out. Not purposely, but because other Hispanic groups knew nothing about the history of New Mexico and its vast contributions in making this country so great. Ignorance about the tremendous imprint of New Mexico on the very fiber of American history has been so prevalent that New Mexico is virtually ignored. New Mexico Latinos have been conveniently cast into the universal label of Mexican American. At some points, ironically, American writers have used this misnomer to describe all Latinos, no matter where they come from, calling all North Americans and South Americans Mexican.

Spanish colonists settled the vast territory of New Mexico, which included Arizona and parts of the present states of California, Nevada, Colorado and Texas, in 1598. The majority of these pioneering settlers were Spanish families that had arrived directly from Spain, or families that had migrated to New Spain (Mexico) at an earlier date. Spanish soldiers who protected the colonists brought their families. Franciscan friars who were determined to do missionary work among the Indians also journeyed to the new settlement.

Las Llaves (The Keys), mixed media by Rosalinda Pacheco. Grandmothers always held hidden knowledge that they opened up with their own set of keys.

Some Indians from Mexico who were servants and laborers accompanied the settlers. A Pueblo Indian revolt took place in 1680, wherein revolting Indians spearheaded by an Indian medicine man named Popé massacred a large number of the colonists and priests and slaughtered Christianized Pueblo Indians. Spanish colonists, along with escaping Indians, were exiled to an area called El Paso del Norte until 1692–93, when some Indians and Spanish returned to New Mexico and resettled.

From the eighteenth century onward, New Mexico with its capital city in Santa Fe was a central power of influence in the region. Contrary to what has been written, New Mexico was not isolated. Spanish government was maintained. Most of the settlers were highly literate, so official documents and letters were written in the language of the times. Books were also available in the colonies.

It is interesting that many historians and scholars of American studies appear to fail in uncovering many interesting details of New Mexico and United States history. For example, everyone at one time or another has learned about the famous Meriwether Lewis and William Clark expedition, but few know the two were involved in a spying mission into Spanish territory. It is also not often mentioned what happened to the principals in that mission. Richard Edwards and M. Hopewell, MD, wrote in their book *Great West* (1860):

> *In the first part of autumn, 1809, an event took place, which caused a universal gloom among the inhabitants, and many a weeping eye in St. Louis distilled drops of anguish for the death of a magistrate, friend, and statesman. For many months Governor Meriwether Lewis had been subject to mental depression, without having any visible cause for his melancholy. His friends viewed the marked change in his conduct with disquietude, and bestowed upon him those thousand little attentions which respect and warm friendship will suggest, and all in vain. While on a journey, (he was proceeding to Louisville) Governor Lewis deliberately ended his life with his pistol. He was a man of energy, probity and ambition; had received the most marked tokens of his country's approbation, and was universally beloved. What was the fountain source of that melancholy madness, which induced him to perform such shuddering deed, is a myth at the present day. His disposition from a youth was pensive—inclined to be "moody from his earliest day." It has been suggested that Meriwether Lewis was stricken with*

Navajo Hogan, dwelling built of mud and wood pine logs in New Mexico. Hogans were not only homes but also spiritual residences.

grief by what he and Clark had done to the Indians including Sacajawea during their famous explorations of Spanish territory. Historians some times only provide and record bits and pieces of history, not thinking about the relevance of material that actually affected the lives of people.

Once the Santa Fe Trail opened up around 1825, trade and commerce between New Mexico and the United States through Missouri took place. This was a boon not only for New Mexico traders, farmers and ranchers, but for the overall economy as well. However, New Mexicans were not accustomed to the wasteful ways of the Americans who entered into the territory. In the United States, many people were used to the misuse of natural resources and the killing of wildlife, sometimes for sport. New Mexico Hispanics and the Indians made use of everything. For example, when a buffalo was slaughtered, every single piece of the animal was used. Americans killed buffalo to subjugate the Indians or to get the Indians out of the way through starvation.

People traveling on wagon trains to Santa Fe from Missouri threw away the tin cans that were coming into use for fruits, vegetables and other commodities. New Mexico tinsmiths picked the tin cans up and produced beautiful frames for religious images imported from the East and tabernacles to house locally produced wooden religious statues. In time, the tinsmiths used the tin from cans for many other items, including boxes and candlesticks. American immigrants on the trail disposed of anything they felt was no longer necessary or needed. New Mexicans used scraps of wood and bits of cloth, including cotton and gunnysacks. Pieces of wallpaper and even shipping crates were salvaged. The folk art that was produced with these items is prized in the collectible market. Aside from what has been written down in New Mexico history books, little is actually known about what happened behind the scenes. For example, Stephen Watts Kearny and his Missouri forces that invaded New Mexico in 1846 are treated lightly. Nothing else is written other than the preferential history. But there are more interesting notes to New Mexico history, such as the following.

Edwards and Hopewell stated that on June 22, 1848,

The country was called upon to mourn the death of General Stephen W. Kearny, who died of chronic diarrhea…that proved more fatal to our gallant officers and soldiers than the arms of the enemies. General Kearny was a native of New Jersey, and when in the eighteenth year of his age, and when a student of Nassau Hall, Princeton, at the breaking out of the war

An Indian chief and spiritual leader supervise a group of dancers. Sacred dances performed for centuries maintained closeness between this world and the next.

in 1812 with Great Britain, he obtained a commission of first-lieutenant. He was taken prisoner during the war....Having thus early entered upon the profession of arms...until he was cut off by death, in the fifty-fifth year of his age...Colonel Kearny...was sent to protect the frontier parts of the western country, which for many years were visited with all the horrors of savage warfare. He was engaged in the campaign in the south against the Comanches....He kept the frontier settlements free from those terrible atrocities, which form the record of most of the pioneer settlements of our land. He married Miss Radford, stepdaughter of Gov. William Clark in St. Louis; and during the Mexican war, with the rank of brigadier-general, by order of the government [the government of Missouri, not United States] *he went across "the plains" to take possession of Mexico and California. History has recorded his success in accomplishing the responsible mission confided to him. The city of St. Louis was his home; and he was buried with military honors...an impressive sermon was delivered on the occasion by the Rev. Bishop Hawks...Then when the body was deposited in the vault, the artillery boomed, and three rounds were fired by the infantry; then the procession started for the city, and the remains of the lamented Kearny were left in the cemetery.*

Unfortunately, much about what has been written about New Mexico history in the past has been tainted by half-truths, misinformation, prejudice and bias. Very few know that during the American Revolution, New Mexico Spanish presidio soldiers provided a part of their salaries to help with the War of Independence in 1776. Most others are unaware that if it were not for the trade on the Santa Fe Trail, from about 1820 to the late 1800s, the U.S. economy might have collapsed. History books fail to mention that New Mexico played a pivotal role in saving the Union during the Civil War. President Jefferson Davis and his military advisors suggested that taking over the territory of New Mexico was of extreme importance. Conquering that area would be taking over the rich gold fields in Colorado. The Confederacy could have ports for ships to deliver supplies and goods on the West Coast. The benefits would, most certainly, be immense. What was unexpected was that around twelve thousand Hispanic New Mexicans would volunteer to fight for the North. These extremely brave men and their families provided their own armaments, food supplies, horses and goods. Spanish territories had outlawed slavery. New Mexico Hispanics followed suit by going against the Confederacy. Lieutenant Colonel Manuel Antonio Chávez y Noriega led a group of New Mexico volunteers that defeated the Confederates at the famous Battle of Glorieta and saved the West for the Union.

This is only a part of the history. Most know little, or next to nothing, about the very mysterious history of the Land of Enchantment—a land that bewitches you and casts a never-ending spell on all who see it. Everyone is enraptured and delighted by what is found. This is especially true when an unexpected discovery leads to captivating, fascinating and bizarre pieces of mystifying heritage and unexplained history. There is a surge in COVID-19 affecting New Mexico and the rest of the country. New Mexico newspapers try to equate this new epidemic with the national influenza pandemic of 1918–19. Writers have covered only a part of the story. What is left out is the significant role that New Mexico's *curanderas*, or medicine women, played in New Mexico during this devastating period. It is estimated that over seventeen million and perhaps closer to one hundred million died worldwide at this time.

In New Mexico, when doctors simply gave up, curanderas selflessly treated patients. These New Mexico Spanish women were not witch doctors using feathers, brush and plants while calling on spiritual gods to heal as some have written. New Mexico curanderas were extremely knowledgeable about medicinal herbs, roots and plants. Interestingly, many of these natural

Left to right: Felicitas Vallejos Calles, Sinforosa Márquez and Dolores Márquez. Nana Felicitas always shared supernatural and paranormal stories with her daughter and granddaughter.

medicinal compounds are found today in modern medicine. In my family, it was said that my great-grandmother Doña Catalina Mondragón de Valdez, who was a famous curandera in northern New Mexico, saved many lives during this period. What was her remedy? She used dried *hierba buena* (spearmint) leaves and the dried flowers of the *plumajillo* plant. Plumajillo, commonly called yarrow, is *Achillea millefolium*, a plant found in New Mexico. Indians used this plant in many forms to break fever. My mother would grind these two plants together into a powder, mix these up with lard to create a paste and apply this to the body, which then had to be completely covered up. My great-grandmother would then slice potatoes, dip them in vinegar, and then place them in a cloth that was tied around the forehead. High fevers dissipated. The patients followed up by drinking plenty of tea made from the chamomile plant. Those who were ill were cured. People in New Mexico firmly believed in miracles.

Researchers have always been wondering why ancient Indian villages in New Mexico were mysteriously abandoned hundreds of years before the Spanish arrived. Skeletal remains could not be found. How could thriving people suddenly leave their ancient dwellings without any explanation? It is now thought and written that Indians in New Mexico destroyed anything and everything that was associated with the person who lived. Even those who took bodies out into far-out areas took their clothing off when they returned to the village and burned them. Anything the deceased had touched was destroyed and burned. Not even the names of those who had lived could be uttered in thoughts of the deceased. There is a famous saying that history repeats itself. Eerie happenings were a natural occurrence in the daily lives of New Mexicans. This was to be expected, especially in a land in which one could be enraptured and entranced. Perhaps what ancient ancestors in New Mexico experienced was not altogether mysterious but an explanation of ancient pandemics and natural occurrences. Things that totally confound present-day experts studying the past will be found to actually exist.

FORWARD INTO THE UNKNOWN

An ethereal wind sweeps through a person's soul, until it returns as a shadow.

The Angel of Darkness is coming. Waiting to get you! When can we have our first encounter with things we don't understand? For me, it was as an infant lying in my crib late at night. Some things we never forget. I was scared. I didn't know why. All I knew was something in the darkness was trying to reach out for me. I didn't cry. My crib was very close to my parents' bed, so the first time this happened, I reached out with my little hand for my father's strong hand. When he held my hand with his, I could sleep. I felt secure and that whatever was out there in the dark could not get to me.

Current research claims there are some people who do have the ability to recollect events from their infancy and early childhood. Researchers have gone as far as to say that some claim to remember certain things from the time they were in their mother's womb. I do recall vividly that before I could even walk, while sitting in my high chair in the kitchen, I remember crawling on the floor while going around exploring. When I first started school, I told my mother that I had been at her and my father's wedding reception. They were married in 1933. I was born in 1946. I described the reception by telling her it was a long hall. I saw the musicians at the front of the room. I told her that the men and boys wore dark suits and were sitting on wooden benches to one side of the room, and the women and girls, wearing light-colored dresses, sat on benches on the opposite side. When the musicians began to play traditional Spanish New Mexican songs with guitars and violins, the men crossed over to dance with the women. Some of the old men sat with gnarled wood canes between their legs, and when the music began, they rhythmically tapped their canes on the floor while they kept up with the beat. This scene was very clear in my mind, and when I told this story to my mother, María Cleofas, she laughed, but then she was perplexed. As I grew older, I learned many curious supernatural things about our culture and heard many mystifying stories from my mother. She came from a little village called Peñasco Blanco, near Mora, New Mexico. My mother was from a family of twelve children—six boys and six girls. What was most interesting about my mother is that she was extremely superstitious. She had an ingrained fear of witches and spirits.

My mother warned me about *duendes*, little goblins that can appear late at night. She told me that these creatures could come out from hiding and cause terrifying havoc. While we were sleeping, duendes could creep out and pull at our toes. My older sister was terrified about these nocturnal goblins. She couldn't sleep comfortably unless she tied the sheets around her feet so that the duendes couldn't get at her toes. My mother told me about being careful not to go to the Arroyo Manteca, near our home. This was a ditch that channeled water from the Creston Mountains nearby. She warned that if I went there, La Llorona, a woman who lived long ago that lost her children, might think I was one of her kids and she might take me. My mother said this crying, wandering woman is in an endless search for her children that drowned. She went into the waters trying to save them and drowned. Her spirit rose up, and La Llorona appears late at night, searching for her lost children near waterways.

My family and I lived in a two-story house in Las Vegas, New Mexico. In time, I found out our home, Adlon House, was haunted. It had an interesting history tied to the Adlon family. Charles Adlon and his elderly parents, Josef and Demetria, immigrated to the United States from Germany around 1882. They settled down in Las Vegas. Charles established Adlon Iron Works, where he produced iron hitching posts for horses, railings for homes and cemeteries and decorations also for cemeteries. He had a very successful business. His aunt Emma Adlon joined them in Las Vegas. She was an artist who became successful by painting portraits and western scenes of cowboys and Indians. The family was quite happy, but after the turn of the twentieth century, Charles's old parents passed away. Aunt Emma comforted Charles. One day while at his shop, something changed Charles Adlon's life. A much younger woman named Adelina Hays walked in, asking for a job. He hired her immediately. After a time, they fell in love and were married although

Maximo de Aragón and Adelina Hays Adlon. Adelina was the widow of Charles Adlon. After Adelina's death, her spirit and Charles's ghost appeared at Adlon House.

Charles was around thirty-five years older. For their honeymoon, Charles told Adelina he would give her two choices. She could choose between a trip to Europe or a new home. She chose a new home. This house was built in 1921 on North Pacific Street, which was renamed Hot Springs Boulevard. It was a boulevard of broken dreams and nightmares.

My father, Maximiliano de Aragón, whom they called Maximo, or Max, told me Adlon House was built with two thousand *terrones*, which are twice as large as an average adobe brick. The house was two stories high with two-foot-thick walls in some places. After about a year, Charles and Adelina's son Edwin was born. Later on, Charles died unexpectedly in an upstairs bedroom. A room they called *el cuarto largo*—meaning "long room"—about twenty feet wide by fifty feet long was adjacent to an alley where Adelina set up a photography studio she called Adlon Photography. This is how she provided for herself and her infant son. One day, my nineteen-year-old father went to the studio to have his picture taken. She took several shots of him posing in different positions. They were not average photos. He liked flexing his muscles and showing off. They wound up dating and were married at

Saint Francis Cathedral in Santa Fe, New Mexico, on July 10, 1924. Father Eliguis Kumelcel, as the rector of the cathedral, officiated at the wedding. The witnesses were Father Roger Aull and Oscar Fries. My father always spoke to me about dancing the Charleston and the Black Bottom at the reception held at the La Fonda Hotel across the street from the cathedral. "It was really the Roaring Twenties," he said. He was twenty-one years old.

Max wound up working for the Republic Insurance Company, which had a main office in Denver, Colorado. A few years later, he had a business trip to Denver. When he returned from the trip, he couldn't find Adelina at home or anywhere nearby. Someone told him she had to be taken to the Las Vegas Hospital for an emergency. When Max got to the hospital, he found Edwin crying in the waiting room. The little boy was now nine years old. Adelina died from a ruptured appendix. The wake was held at the house, and her body lay in state in an elaborate coffin next to the dining room. She was laid to rest at Mount Calvary Cemetery. The night of the funeral, my father and his little stepson went to bed in a long room located above the staircase. He tried to comfort his stepson, who kept weeping. My father assured his little stepson that he would take care of him. Suddenly, a white lace curtain in front of the window at the foot of the bed began to sway lightly in the moonlight. My father thought nothing of it. He thought he might have left the window, which overlooked the street below, a little open. The swaying curtain's movement from side to side and back and forth continued. Once in a while, they could hear a car on the street or someone walking in the alley. Their eyes stayed riveted on the curtain as they spoke about the sad events of the day.

Then the curtain flew up, and Adelina stood at the foot of the bed. She looked down at them. They were both terrified. She had died, yet she was there. Adelina didn't speak. She just looked at them with wide, pain-filled eyes. My father and Edwin were frozen with fear as her sad spirit disappeared. She never returned, but the ghost of Charles Adlon did. Many stories were told. I was always interested in listening to them. According to my mother, Adlon's spirit would appear for a period, every ten years. Several people, including my older sister and brother, an aunt and other family and visitors who slept at our house, claimed to have seen him at night. The most astonishing account was related to my father by his stepson, Edwin Adlon.

When I was in third grade, Edwin and his son Darren arrived for a visit. My father owned another house right next to the Adlon House, so we were living there. Edwin's career was that of a jeweler. He lived

Maximo de Aragón, stepson Edwin Adlon and Ramona Hernández. When Adelina Adlon, Maximo's wife, passed away, she appeared to him and Edwin after the funeral.

in Albuquerque and stopped by for a visit. I was quite happy with his visits because he always gave my brother and me gifts. I never forgot that he gave my older brother and me Hopalong Cassidy pocketknives. I treasured mine. Edwin asked my father if he could have the key to the other house so he and his son could sleep there, and my father gave it to him. He chose an upstairs bedroom to sleep in. Darren decided to go for a ride around town, so Edwin went to bed. When he started dozing off, he heard footsteps in the hallway. Edwin was certain his son had returned. Then he saw someone standing at the doorway. It wasn't his son. Edwin called out, "Who is it?" but there was no answer. The person across the room just stared at him. Then Edwin said, "My name is Edwin Adlon, son of Charles Adlon." Then there were other footsteps in the hall, and the bizarre figure disappeared. My father related that Edwin and Darren left and stayed at a motel. The next day, Edwin went to pray for hours at his father's grave at the cemetery. He was certain he had appeared to him the night before. Edwin never returned to Las Vegas.

Father Hubert Lomme, pastor at the nearby church of Our Lady of Sorrows, was a frequent visitor at our house when I was a little boy. I remember that at one time he showed up and, after a deep conversation with my parents, went from room to room in our house. He chanted a litany of prayers and sprinkled holy water in each room. It wasn't until I got older that I realized the he had performed an exorcism at our house. The determined priest sought to expel the peculiar spirit that lurked in our home, I later learned, by saying,

Monsignor Hubert Lomme, pastor of Our Lady of Sorrows Church in Las Vegas, New Mexico, performed an exorcism at Adlon House. The spirit continued.

> *Most glorious prince of the Heavenly Armies, Saint Michael the Archangel, defend us in our battle against the rulers of the world of darkness, against evil spirits....Take hold of the dragon, the ancient serpent, which is the devil and Satan....Bind him and cast him into the bottomless pit....As wax melts before the fire, so the wicked perish in the presence of God.... We drive you from us, wherever you may be, unclean spirit....May you be snatched away and be driven from this house.*

Apparently, this astounding religious ritual did not work. My father recalled when a man who bullied everyone at the plaza was returning home from a late night out on the town. As he rounded the corner to walk through the alley behind the house, he saw a tall man standing and leaning up against a back wall. The bully was taken aback by the odd presence. He asked, "Who are you?" The glaring man did not answer. Drawing a pistol from his coat pocket, he yelled out, "Tell me who you are, or I'll shoot you!" The mysterious figure was still motionless. The stunned bully fired until his pistol was empty. The brazen man just stood there staring at the bully, who then tossed his gun and ran away like a maniac. My father said the bully became a changed man. One time he took me to look at the wall and asked what I could see. I saw holes in the wall. My father told me to count the holes. There were six.

When I was about seventeen years old, attending Robertson High School, I slept in the large master bedroom near my parents on a Hollywood bed. This was to conserve heat during the cold winter. One night, I woke up to the presence of someone standing next to my bed. I instinctively knew it was someone who meant to harm me. I tried to call my parents for help, but for some strange reason, I couldn't speak. Not a single sound came out from my mouth. I didn't know what to do. I tried to calm myself down. The only thing I could think of was to grunt as loud as I could. I grunted louder. This sound woke my father up, and he asked in a loud voice, "What's wrong?" When I heard his voice, the presence immediately left the room and I felt safe.

My mother often talked about an experience she once had in Adlon House. My father was a salesman who was always traveling throughout New Mexico. He sold many items to neighborhood grocery stores. He started his business during World War II and was quite successful. There was a day when he was gone and was scheduled to return home. I was at school, as was my older brother. My sister was also out of our home. My mother said she was washing dishes in the kitchen when she heard the furniture moving in the dining room, and the dishes were rattling in the china cabinet. She was stunned. My mother said she walked into the dining room to see what was going on. When she stepped into the dining room, the sounds stopped. She went back into the kitchen to continue washing dishes. She thought the sounds were nothing more than her imagination, but when my mother went to the kitchen sink, she heard the same sounds. She said she walked out of the house until my father returned home moments later. She frantically told him about what happened. She said he went to every room in the house and checked all of the windows. He found nothing.

My older sister always played her piano in the living room, next to the dining room. When I was a little boy, I enjoyed sitting next to her just to hear her play. We often sang songs as she played. On top of the piano, there was a timer that swung back and forth. My sister would release the timer as she played her tunes. I loved the sounds of the metronome and the music coming from the ivory keys. My sister said that when we were all gone from the house and she was alone in her upstairs bedroom, she heard the piano playing downstairs. Her first thought was that someone we knew had come into the house and was playing the piano. When she walked down the stairs to check it out, the playing stopped when she was close to reaching the bottom of the stairs. Like my mother, she felt it was her imagination. She went back to her bedroom. The piano playing started again. When we got home, she was frantic. Once again, my dad checked every room and every window and found nothing. The timer, however, was swinging back and forth.

After the terrible episode when I lost my breath and felt my father saved me, we moved upstairs. We slept in a long room next to the stairway. My parents slept on a bed near the window where Adelina Adlon had appeared at the foot of the bed. I slept farther away. I got used to sleeping right up against the wall next to my bed. I left part of my pillow sticking out and placed my rosary on that part of the pillow. I woke up one night and felt that someone was standing next to my bed. I knew that the rosary protected me, so I was not afraid. Although it was dark and I couldn't see, I knew this person would raise a hand and strike the pillow. It happened. Then it was gone. I rested secure knowing my rosary had protected me.

The following morning, my parents were having breakfast in the kitchen. They were both drinking coffee. I walked in and served myself a bowl of cereal. When I sat down, my mother was telling my father,

> *Something very strange happened last night. I woke up in the middle of the night. I heard footsteps on the stairs, and when I looked, someone was standing at the doorway. Although it was dark, I could see a lighted-up face. The person had a blank stare. After a few steps, this person walked toward our son's bed and stood next to it. I tried to wake you up but I couldn't say anything! I started praying and calling on all of the saints. The person turned around and walked down the stairs. I heard a loud thud where we have a painting of the crucifixion hanging on the wall down the stairs.*

How could a similar event happen to two separate people, I thought. Did I imagine it? Did she?

My father always talked about mysterious balls of fire that suddenly appear. My mother said that when *bolas de lumbre* (balls of fire) appear, they are witches that have transformed themselves into flames of fire and go about dancing. She showed me an area near South Pacific Street in Las Vegas near some foothills. She claimed balls of fire that had transformed into witches were seen there. My father's take was that if you saw a ball of fire, it could lead you to a treasure. This was a long-held belief in New Mexico. He said he saw a ball of fire in our house one night and followed it. Then it went down into the floor at the foot of the stairs. My dad claimed that the next day, he crawled under the house and tried to dig. After several hours, he found nothing. The next story, perhaps, would lead to a treasure.

A business owner in San Juan, a village near San Jose—by Bernal and Villanueva, near Las Vegas—had an interesting story to tell. He told my father that one night he saw a bola de lumbre and followed it. The lighted-up ball traveled slowly, he said, and then went into the ground some yards away. He was certain there was a treasure there. My father had purchased one of the first ore locators that was produced in the 1950s. I was a kid and accompanied my father and my older brother to San Juan. We picked the storeowner up, and he led us on the trail to riches. After following an isolated trail, we finally arrived at the spot he said that the ball of fire went down. My dad took out his ore detector, which was an early metal detector, and started working. One beep on the old detector followed another. They started to dig. Excitement grew as the machine started going wild. I sat on a large rock and watched my dad, his friend and my brother in amazement. After an hour or so, they were ready to give up. They had found no treasure. The grocery store owner prodded them on, saying, "This is where the bola de lumbre went down. There has to be a treasure here."

They kept digging. One spade full of dirt followed another. Then they found curious stones that were shaped like little crosses. They tossed them away. I picked some up. I found them to be pretty and interesting. They finally gave up and were enormously discouraged at finding no treasure. Many years later, after my father passed away, I discovered they had found staurolite crosses in crystal. People call these curious rocks fairy stones. These cross-like pieces of stone were embedded with garnets. It is written that the rocks have shapes similar to the Saint Andrew's cross, or ancient Roman crosses. Some are shaped like the Maltese cross. My poor father, my brother and the insistent storeowner found a treasure, and they didn't know it! The little stones sell for ten to twenty dollars apiece in today's market.

After I graduated from high school in 1964, we moved to Albuquerque. I enlisted in the New Mexico Air National Guard, affectionately called the "Enchilada Air Force," in 1966. Al Sánchez was my recruiter. His brothers, whom everyone at Kirtland Air Force Base called Tiny Morrie and Baby Gaby, also worked at the main office. My fellow recruits included Roberto Griego, Guy Jacobus, Jake Montaño, Joe Bravo and Richard Romero, and I loved playing ping-pong with them during our breaks. The Sánchez brothers were hard to beat. The three formed the well-known Al Hurricane Band. In 1967, I joined Reies López Tijerina's civil rights movement. These were highlights in my life, but a more significant one was to follow.

I was always very interested in unidentified flying objects, UFOs. My mother told me that she and my dad would often see saucer-shaped objects flying in the sky above in our hometown of Las Vegas, New Mexico. Many people, including my parents, would see these objects flying in *V* formations in the sky above Las Vegas right after World War II. I often wished that I could have seen something like that, especially when I read about the Roswell incident and other sightings around New Mexico.

On a hot summer night in 1967, I decided to go for a ride in my car. As I drove near Old Town in Albuquerque, I lowered my window because of the heat. On a side street near the park, I glanced at the Sandia Mountains. It was a bright, starry night. A falling meteorite caught my attention. When it suddenly stopped above the mountains, I decided to pull over. The bright object darted in a southwesterly direction at a very high speed and then stopped and suddenly reverted back to its original position. It stayed suspended in the air for a few minutes. Being in the air force, I knew this was not a conventional aircraft. After a minute, the maneuvers from this object defied all rational explanations. It flew up and down in zigzag patterns. It then returned once again to its original position in the air. The bright object seemed to go against what we know about gravity and all explained natural phenomena. Then this object flew at an incredible speed across the sky, and it disappeared within a matter of seconds. I was completely stunned.

A couple of months after this, I was back in my hometown of Las Vegas. I picked up my friend David Trujillo, and we went for a ride around town and then decided to drive out to Storrie Lake. I picked out a spot; we parked and had a conversation about life and our futures. Once again, the night sky was brilliant and full of clear stars. I saw a meteorite falling and called David's attention to see it. Then this bright object suddenly stopped. We were both stunned. David and I studied the object, which then darted across the sky at an incredible speed, disappearing in the horizon. Seconds later, an airliner appeared, flying at regular speeds. This aircraft was slow and deliberate, and it took minutes to cross the sky. I wrote an article about these sightings, and it was published in a national UFO magazine.

In 1968, I was deployed to serve on active duty in the U.S. Air Force. I was sent to Eglin Air Force Base in Florida. I spent two months training with the 560th Civil Engineering Squadron, Red Horse Unit. Nothing eventful took place other than making it through the obstacle courses and a twenty-mile hike with a loaded backpack. One weekend, my companions and I decided to drive out to the Castillo de San Marcos, the Spanish colonial fortress (1672–1696) located along Matanzas Bay. After crossing a long bridge, I suddenly knew which streets we would turn on and in which direction we were going before we would get there. It was as if I had already been there before. It was a strange feeling. What was even stranger was that I knew the names of the streets and words on signs before I saw them. It was a mystery I couldn't explain to myself.

After I was married in 1972, my wife and I moved to my hometown of Las Vegas. My father passed away in 1976. A few weeks after the funeral, my brother, Max, and I sat in the living room of our parents' home, reminiscing about our dad. It was late at night, and when we stopped talking, we both heard someone trying to open a back door. We heard the latch open and someone walk in. There were about ten steps. Then we heard a drawer being pulled open and someone thumbing through some papers. The drawer was then closed, and this person walked out of the room. My brother and I immediately got up and went to check. The door was locked. We checked the sounds of the door being unlatched, the number of steps, the drawer opening and closing, the return steps and the door being closed and latched. Everything checked out. When we looked into the drawer, the papers inside belonged to our father.

On another night, I was in the kitchen next to the table. I saw a bright, luminous light moving slowly through the living room. It was the shape of a globe, about the size of a basketball. It is hard to describe, but it was an ethereal light, not blinding but soft. It was a bright orb that appeared to emit luminous rays from within. The second I saw it, I felt it was nothing to be afraid of. It was calming and reassuring. I studied the orb as it traveled, and it went right through the wall. I instinctively ran out through the front door and to the back of our house to discover if I could see it. The luminous light had disappeared. It was then and there that I knew what both of my parents had talked about. Scientists have described these phenomena as ball lightning and other natural occurrences. For centuries, the lights have been written about and reported throughout the world. They have been referred to as Saint Elmo's Fires and by many other names. Scientists claim these mysterious lights appear during and after a rainstorm, but they do not know their actual origin.

Around 1995, my wife, Rosa, and I and our daughters, Lucia and Linda, drove out to see the Spanish colonial mission ruins of Abo near Mountainair. This site, along with Quarai and other ruins, figured in a number of mysterious appearances in seventeenth-century New Mexico. (These unusual paranormal sightings are explored further in this book.) When we got out of the car and walked to the mission ruins, I had a strange feeling the moment I stepped through the ruined doorway of the ancient church. In this hallowed ground, I experienced an emotional aura. I was immediately stunned as I stood there in the midst of the massive ruins. I could feel a presence as I viewed the impressive structure. After we left, it was some time later that I found out that both my wife and Lucia had a similar experience.

Our family enjoyed visiting the ruins of Abo, and I had read about the mysterious painting housed at the San Francisco de Asis Catholic Church at Ranchos de Taos. The site of our next trip was to visit the beautiful and iconic Spanish colonial church. It was completed around 1815 and is a National Historic Landmark. A special attraction at the church is a painting known as *The Shadow of the Cross*. French Canadian artist Henry Ault produced this eight-foot oil on canvas in 1896. The artist went to bed after he completed his faithful work of Christ standing on the shore of the Sea of Galilee. He was awakened in the middle of the night by a light coming from his studio. Ault was amazed when he saw his painting glowing in the dark. Others saw the painting and questioned him about its lighting up. Henry Ault always proclaimed he could not explain why his art piece lit up in the darkness.

The Shadow of the Cross was exhibited at the 1904 World's Fair in St. Louis, Missouri. The painting caused a sensation among thousands of viewers. It was eventually donated to the Taos church around 1948. "I can't explain it, Father Tim Martinez said. "I don't know if it's a miracle or not. It is a mystery. Anyone can see it for what it is to them." My family and I have now seen this unusual painting several times. We sat down on folding chairs in the room with the painting directly in front of us. Understandably, I was skeptical at first. All of us listened to an introduction giving a brief history of the odd painting. Then the presenter said, "Prepare yourselves for a mystery no one can explain." We were instructed to look at the painting and study it. I saw a painting, a beautiful work that displayed the heartfelt and deep devotion of the artist. The lights were then turned off. After minutes, my eyes adjusted to the darkness. I saw nothing. Then, the painting began to glow. It had a mindboggling steady luminescence. Clouds that I saw earlier were more defined in the dark. A cross gradually appeared next to Christ's shoulder and then a fishing boat became apparent. Then a halo appeared. I felt as though I was in the presence of something beyond our comprehension. They say scientists from Los Alamos National Labs examined the painting, and they couldn't explain how it glows in the dark since it was created when glow-in-the-dark paint didn't exist. There is another mystery that always intrigued me.

Left: *The Shadow of the Cross*, 1896 painting by Henri Ault at Ranchos de Taos Church. During daylight, Christ is at the Sea of Galilee. *Courtesy of Father Tim Martínez, former pastor of San Francisco de Asis Church.*

Right: The *Shadow* painting mysteriously luminesces in darkness and a cross and boat appear. *Courtesy of Father Tim Martínez, former pastor of San Francisco de Asis Church.*

I read an article about a rising coffin at the church of Isleta Pueblo. An *Albuquerque Journal* reporter wrote that the coffin inexplicably rises up through the depths of the ground. When it is reburied, the coffin rises up again at different times. This story stayed in the back of my mind until the fall of 2015, when I decided to research the tale and write about it. After an in-depth investigation, I discovered a story that was a combination of history, fact and fiction. The basic evidence revolves around a martyred priest named Fray Juan de Padilla. He accompanied the Francisco Vazquez de Coronado expedition of 1540 that searched for the fabled Seven Cities of Gold. According to Indian legend, this land of unimaginable riches lay somewhere in New Mexico territory. Fray de Padilla stayed behind to minister to the Indians. He converted some of the tribes to Catholicism but died at

Fray Francisco Juan de Padilla, eighteenth-century engraving. Fray de Padilla accompanied the Coronado Expedition in 1540 and was martyred. His coffin rises, and his spirit appears.

the hands of warring Indians when he attempted to save those who were traveling with him. His body was put into a hollowed-out cottonwood tree and placed in a cave. The fray's remains were apparently later transferred to the mission church of San Agustin de la Isleta, built in 1613 at Isleta Pueblo. It is here that history and fiction gets mixed up.

The Indians at the pueblo forgot whose body was buried in the church. According to legend, it was someone with some powers that could have been bad. The Pueblo Indian Revolt of 1680 may have contributed to the

A crowd rushes to Isleta Pueblo mission church to see the remains of Fray Juan de Padilla and his sensational "rising coffin," 1909. Photo by Williamson Haffner Company.

confusion. Isleta Indians left with the retreating Spanish colonists to escape the wrath of Popé and his followers, who were terrorizing, killing and pillaging in the territory. Some Isleta Indians returned to their ancestral pueblo in 1692, but it wasn't until the late eighteenth century that the fray's remains were disinterred and examined. De Padilla's remains were incorruptible—this means his body had not decomposed. Church officials examined the remains at different periods of history, and parts of the body were found to be missing. According to tradition, in the late nineteenth century, some of the Indians were dancing in the church during a pueblo festival. While dancing, they heard a rumble on the floor. The noise got increasingly louder. Then they said a coffin rose up to the level of the floor as the altar shook. The Indian dancers were frightened. They ran out the door, and the story spread.

The story about the rising coffin at Isleta traveled far and wide. The tale grew in popularity and in mystery because the coffin rose at different times through the years. No one could explain what was happening. How could a coffin be buried six feet or more under the dirt and then rise to the top of the ground? Experts attempted to offer a variety of explanations. One theory was that during the flooding of the Rio Grande River a quarter of a mile or more away, water seeped under the coffin and steadily pushed it up. But the coffin rose even during periods of severe drought. Plus, no other coffins buried nearby rose up. Perhaps the dancing on the hard-packed dirt floor pushed the coffin up. This was plausible, but the coffin rose up even when all dancing in the church ceased taking place. Then theorists debated who was buried in this coffin. The coffin had been replaced through the years due to the deterioration of the original hollowed-out tree. Experts didn't think the remains were those of Fray Juan de Padilla. Perhaps they were the remains of another priest who had ministered at the Isleta church, they thought. No one could agree on anything, especially why the coffin rose up.

Debate and confusion clouded the story of the rising coffin at Isleta Pueblo. During the 1920s, a French priest by the name of Father Anton Docher served as the pastor at Isleta. He became obsessed with the case of Fray Juan de Padilla. The priest reportedly spent sleepless nights investigating everything that had to do with this strange story. However, Father Docher was seriously injured, purportedly while attempting to open up the coffin with the remains of the fray to study the body. He intended to put it on display in the church for religious veneration. Father Anton was convinced this martyred fray was not only a saint, but that everyone in the Catholic Church of New Mexico should know about him as well. Father Docher's arm would have to be amputated because gangrene set in. The devoted priest prayed to the fray instead, and a miracle took place. He was completely and inexplicably cured. This was one of several miracles attributed to Fray Juan de Padilla. Church officials at the Archdiocese of Santa Fe, including Archbishop Edwin P. Byrne, were asked to look into Fray Juan de Padilla,

As archbishop of Santa Fe, Bishop Edward Vincent Byrne (*second from right*) ordered pouring of cement over the rising coffin of Fray de Padilla.

buried in this oldest surviving mission church in the United States. In the end, who was buried there? Church experts weighed in, and the archdiocese decided to quash the sainthood case of a Spanish missionary in New Mexico because it couldn't be conclusively decided whose remains were interred at this church. Concrete was poured over the grave without any fanfare so that the coffin couldn't rise up again. The church officially closed the mysterious case of the rising coffin and the controversy was buried.

I relate my experiences and those of others with the supernatural and the mysterious because New Mexico history is replete with similar stories. There are unnatural dimensions in existence in the world we can't explain. I include some of this lore in this book. Skeptics easily dismiss archaeological artifacts and structures that do not fit into our convenient historical time frames or neat files.

HOMELAND OVERVIEW

El venado y la venada se fueron a Santa Fe,
a vender sus venaditos por azúcar y café.

The male and female deer went to Santa Fe,
to sell their little deer for sugar and coffee

My father, Maximo, was a traveling salesman during World War II, the 1950s and early '60s. He sold merchandise to local grocery stores all over New Mexico. He called his highly successful business New Mexico Enterprises. One of the items he sold was *linimento blanco* (white liniment) used to treat muscle aches and pains. Another item was *Parches Guadalupanos*, a sticky and aromatic cloth with a medication used to treat pains. These could be placed anywhere on the body. He also sold *aceite volcánico*, Dr. McLean's Volcanic Oil, a liquid medication that had been available since the 1840s. The things my father sold were popular, and they sold out quickly. He would go out to isolated Spanish American villages and even Indian pueblos such as San Ildefonso and Isleta. My mother and I went along with him.

When I was about eight or nine years old, we went to a place called La Loma near another small town known as Antón Chico in northern New Mexico. My parents often visited two sisters they called Las Ortegas at La Loma. The Ortega sisters, Alicia and Zoraida, had a large area of land on which they raised sheep. They once showed me a massive Spanish colonial wooden loom on which they wove rugs. I was amazed with the loom and

A Spanish Colonial Penitente morada. The lay religious Catholic confraternity met in special chapels to pray, meditate and perform self-discipline.

studied the various parts manufactured with local pine that was drawn from the nearby hills and mountains. Both sisters carded their own wool, made and dyed the threads with natural dyes and created beautiful weavings. They made a good living with the fabulous multicolored weavings they produced and sold. They used traditional patterns that dated from the eighteenth century. I was used to seeing my mother working on her intricate quilts with pieces of cloth cut from our old clothing, including mine. I also marveled at her large doilies and her stitching on flour sacks she used as dishtowels. Seeing the work these two sisters did always caught my attention.

The high ceilings of the ancient Ortega adobe house also struck me. They were twelve or more feet high. I was awed by what I saw. In each room, there was a canvas-type cloth called *manta* stretched across the ceilings. They hung about a foot down from the sides. These cloths were tied down on the *vigas*, round pine beams that supported the ceilings. Zoraida explained to me that the manta was to catch the dirt that would drop down from the mud roof that protected the house from the snow and rain. I was told that every other month the manta would be carefully removed; dust and dirt was shaken out of the cloth, which was then washed and replaced. There was one peculiar thing that caught my attention. Large framed charcoal portraits housed in wide gilded frames were hung up high on the walls close to the ceiling.

Invisible wires were stretched so that the pictures could be seen from the bottom at an angle. Alicia beamed with joy as she told who the sitters in the images were and their stories. Some had met tragic deaths; others lived to a ripe old age. As a kid, I thought it was kind of neat because I could see all of the pictures from my vantage point. It was as though I was looking straight at faces from the past. Those people were looking down at me.

My parents knew two other elderly women called Las Marquez, the Marquez sisters. Lugarda and Sinforosa also inherited land from their parents. It was an extensive area filled with fruit trees. The sisters canned apples, peaches, pears, cherries and apricots. They also dried fruit. Both sisters sold what they produced, and my parents were customers. They were close friends. I always noticed that back in those days, the first things you would see upon entering homes were framed images of the Holy Family. Beautiful colored lithographic prints from the nineteenth century graced entrances. People most often said, "Mi casa es su casa" (my home is your home). In other words, everyone was told to feel at home. Graciousness was the rule of the day. In fact, Sinforosa and Lugarda Marquez always gave my parents a large box of various fruits, and the Ortega sisters gave them weavings. My parents took along gifts for them as well. At both homes, each room had a cross or a horseshoe hanging above the doorway. The horseshoes were for good luck. The crosses were for protection against evil.

One day on a trip to the Santuario de Chimayo, I was exited to see new places and experience new things. I loved seeing this building because it was so old and there were so many interesting objects. My parents told me it was a very special holy place and that I had to pray and show respect.

From the main chapel, we walked into another room. We passed a wood table that had many religious figures of different sizes. They were all made of wood and painted with subdued colors. I studied the sad and otherworldly faces. In a side of this other room was a hole with dirt that was supposed to be miraculous. In the main part of the room I saw crutches, rosaries, prayer books, religious medals and many other items left by pilgrims. As a little boy, I loved the place. Then one day, my father took us on his business trip to a small town called Antón Chico.

As we drove into Antón Chico, we passed an old mercantile store. My father told me that the old owner had arrived penniless in the area back in the 1890s. He was hired to clear out some falling adobe ruins out in a grass field. After a couple of days of hard work knocking down the thick mud walls, a tin can fell out from behind a wall that was barely standing. The man was stunned when he opened the can. It was filled with gleaming gold

Opposite: The Mysterious Healing Well. Around 1813, a strange light led Penitente Bernardo Abeyta to a buried crucifix. He erected a chapel over the spot.

Above: Healing Room at El Santuario (The Sanctuary) at Chimayo. The prayer room in the sacristy holds crutches and other items from those claiming miraculous healings.

coins. My father told me this man quit his job and some time later opened the successful and popular Abercrombie store. My father always made good sales there. We next drove to a store that looked as though it came straight out of the nineteenth century. It sat up on a rise. Several old men with canes were sitting on hand-hewn wooden benches on a porch. Across the dirt road, I saw an ancient sprawling adobe building sitting near the old church with its wooden crosses and tilting tombstones in the front. My mother told me,

> *That is where your great-grandmother Doña Catalina Mondragón de Valdez once lived. She was a curandera, a healer. She treated and cured people with her remedios. She knew all about medicinal plants and roots that were good for different sicknesses. It is said that Doña Catalina saved people during epidemics that affected the very young and the very old and took many lives. Achaque quiere la muerte para llevarse al enfermo. Death will look for an excuse to take the sick. Catalina's sister Francisquita was a partera. She delivered babies. They became famous in many northern New Mexico villages.*

My mother, María Cleofas Sánchez de Aragón, loved reminiscing about the old days. She had many stories to tell. She was born in 1915, just three years after New Mexico became a state. Her father, Don Filimon Sánchez, became a probate judge for San Miguel County. His brother, Pedro Sánchez, according to family folklore, was the first state representative from San Miguel County. My grandfather's name is engraved on a marble stone acknowledging the founders at the county courthouse. Don Leandro Sánchez, my mother's grandfather, was an attorney during the latter part of the nineteenth century. Her family had a farm and ranch in a place called Peñasco Blanco. Pablita Romero Sánchez was her mother. She was a descendant of distinguished ancestors that included Cristóbal Madrid, who served as a Spanish presidio soldier in Santa Fe and is buried in the San Miguel Church. Cristobal's son Antonio Xavier was also a presidio soldier. He supported the American Revolution against the British with special donations of his monthly salary. Antonio Xavier served under Captain (later Governor) Don Juan Bautista de Anza and participated in his campaigns against the Comanche Indians.

María Cleofas came from a family of twelve—six brothers and six sisters. She recalled that her brothers would help their father tending the horses and livestock and mending the fences while she and her sisters helped their mother. There were many things that brought her a great deal of pleasure in those days. For example, my mother said that they would go up into the nearby hills to gather plants to produce brooms and roots from the *amole* plant to make shampoo for their hair. She said her mother knew how to churn butter, make cheeses, cook and sew. She and her sisters learned from their mother.

When we would visit my grandparents, my grandfather was always sitting next to the front door in a little hallway. He would be dressed in a dark suit, wearing a white shirt and wide silk ties. He was always holding a prayer book and would recite long prayers and chanting in Spanish. My grandmother was always in the kitchen. I loved her beans and chile that she cooked on a large wood stove. She would draw a glass of water for me from a sink that had a red pump that led down into a deep well. I would study her movements as she quickly moved the handle up and down to bring up the water. My mother told me that when a cat cries with a wailing sound at night someone is going to die. I heard one such sorrowful piercing cry from a cat next to the window by the alley alongside our house. The eerie cry kept me awake. The next morning, there was a loud conversation and commotion going on in the kitchen. My grandfather had died. The next time I heard a similar cry was when my grandmother died. I believed my mother. Both times we had to wear black for a year. It was the custom. When someone close died, one had to dress in black for a year. No one could sing, dance or listen to music. Of course, no one had a television, and few had a radio. While visiting relatives as a child, I used outhouses and I joyously bathed in a hot tub near a wood-burning stove.

We had to always pray for the repose of souls. My mother told me as a little boy, "Hay almas que andan penando." (There are souls in search of peace.) When someone passed away, "Que Dios lo tenga en su verdadero descanso," (May God keep him, or her, in his or her true peace) was a commonly uttered phrase. It was a sign of the time and place in which pretty much most everyone firmly believed that if people died unrepentant, their souls were doomed and held here on Earth until they could be saved through prayer. Another belief is that when someone is headed toward death, a higher spirituality provides for us to see and experience things that we normally would not go through during life. Stories were told about the spirits of those who were about to die roaming around at night seeing certain places for the last time. They also see people they loved for a final time before moving on to the afterlife. Everything in existence is interconnected and interrelated between life and death.

My mother always had an altar with religious statues and candles in the house. She would tell me, "Los santos de palo hechos por los santeros son los mas milagrosos." (The wood saints made by a carver of holy statues and retablos [painted panels] are the most miraculous.) You can ask them to intercede for you when you pray.

Around this time, my father took me to a place called San Jose. He had customers there and at a nearby village known as San Juan. San Jose had a central church, and all of the homes surrounded it. The place appealed to me because of how everything had been constructed. Many years later, I learned this was a typical Spanish village built with the architectural elements of the past. It was here that my father introduced me to a *santero*. His name was Juan Sánchez, from Raton, and he was in San Jose visiting relatives. He sold his santos at a store on the plaza in Las Vegas owned by Julius Myer. Someone who could carve religious images out of wood intrigued me. Sánchez showed me the wood he used and his carving tools. This interesting man used pine from the nearby hills. He made his own brushes, *yeso* (powdered gypsum/gesso), natural paints and used pine resin.

Penitente procession photo by E.E. Wentworth Layton, 1905. Flagellants follow penitents pulling maderos, heavy wooden crosses, toward a site, representing the crucifixion of Christ.

As a university student, I made retablos with what I learned as a child to earn extra money, and eventually, I became a santero.

My grandfather and my mother's older brothers were very active members of La Hermandad de Nuestro Padre Jesús Nazareno, the Brotherhood of Our Father Jesus, the Nazarene. This group in New Mexico is more popularly known as Los Penitentes (the Penitents). Penitente origins stem from the early ages of the Catholic Church in Spain and across Europe. Various penitent societies prevalent during the black plagues during the Middle Ages practiced self-flagellation, extreme penitential ceremonies and crucifixion in commemoration of the sufferings of Christ. People believed self-discipline was the only way of atonement for the widespread illness and horrendous deaths that were sweeping the known world. Spanish colonists arriving in New Mexico brought these religious practices along with them when they settled New Mexico. Some of these rituals in the area still exist today along with moradas, isolated buildings where Penitentes hold their meetings and plan for Lent.

My grandmother Pablita Romero de Sánchez was a Carmelita. The women had their own penitential societies and, at one time, their own moradas as well. I will never forget the vivid stories about Holy Week at Peñasco Blanco told by my mother. "The Lenten season was actually sad since we wouldn't see your grandfather and my older brothers for forty days.

I would say goodbye to them, and then would see them in their procession until they disappeared over the hills by our house."

During the following days, the girls did the household chores while other brothers who were not old enough to join the brotherhood chopped wood to cook and heat the house. Sometimes my mother visited with her *comadres* (friends).

> *Things went pretty much as before, but every day we could hear the alabados, the sorrowful hymns my grandfather and the other hermanos sang at the morada. The wailing chants echoed down the valley during the day, and far into the night. Some times we could see the hermanos in the distance at night with their glowing lanterns. When Good Friday would finally arrive, my mother and the other women would dress in black, put on their black shawls and covered their heads. They all had an Encuentro, the encounter between large wooden images of Christ and Nuestra Señora de la Soledad, Our Lady of Solitude, made by a santero. Both santos had wigs made of human hair. They would select a Verónica, a girl with long hair whose hair would be used for the santos. I always wished I had been a Verónica. I let my hair grow long, but they never picked me for this very special honor, which was a very, very old tradition.*

El Encuentro (The Encounter), oil on canvas by Rosa María Calles. Lay confraternity religious perform the Vía Crucis wherein Christ and his sorrow-filled mother meet.

Everyone gathered at the Morada de la Santisima Cruz, the Chapel of the Holy Cross, at the end of Good Friday for the continuation of the Passion play and Tinieblas (the Darkness). Someone was selected to play the role of Christ while two others were the thieves. It is believed that long ago, the one standing in for Christ was actually nailed to a cross, but there is no proof of that. Actual photographs from the late nineteenth century show men hauling long, heavy and massive pine crosses to Monte Calvario, a hill representing Mount Calvary, where Christ was crucified. A *rezador*, someone reciting and singing Vía Crucis *alabados* (songs of praise), led the procession. Hooded barebacked and barefoot men wearing white cotton drawers whipped their backs with whips called *disciplinas* (the disciplines). In 1888, noted photographer Charles F. Lummis photographed a man in a black hood whose body was covered by a large white cotton cloth. This unidentified individual was tied to a cross. He was standing on a platform that extended from this ponderous cross. My mother described the following ritual vividly:

> *At the morada for the Tinieblas* [the tenebrous ceremony] *everyone from miles around gathered. I was a little girl the first time I went, maybe ten or eleven. We all had to take metal washboards, big spoons, metal cooking utensils, everything we could to make loud noises with. Men took chains and other things. Inside at the front of a large windowless room was a life-size wooden statue of Christ carved by a famous santero. There was also a big figure of La Muerte, death riding in a wooden cart, with her bow and arrow. She was called Doña Sebastiana. Right in front of the altar was a Tenebrario. This was a triangular thing made of wood with a base that held fifteen lit candles. Each candle was for the Stations of the Cross. The central one at the top stood for Christ. We all sat down quietly on the hard dirt floor and patiently waited when we went in. My mother and the other women did their penance by wearing gunnysack, sackcloth or horsehide with the hair against their skin under their clothing. We were there for quite a while before the wide, heavy wooden doors suddenly creaked open. The black hooded hermanos followed my father, who was a Hermano Mayor, an elder brother. He led the ceremony by saying, "La muerte y la Pasión de Nuestro Señor Jesucristo es el motivo mas dulce, y mas fuerte que puede mover nuestros corazones.* [The death and passion of Our Lord Jesus Christ is the sweetest and the strongest motive that can move our hearts.] *Calvary is the mountain of the followers of the origin of the Passion of the Savior.*

Flagellant brothers at the end of vía Crucis, the Way of the Cross Passion Lenten observances, New Mexico. Photo by E.E. Wentworth Layton, 1905.

The Brothers and Sisters of the cross know that our Redeemer shed his most precious blood for our salvation. We are the cause of his pain, the cause of his death; we wait for his mercy and pardon." After we went through the Stations of the Cross each candle was blown out until only the one for Christ was still lit. When that one was blown out an uproar followed. Parecía que se iba a acabar el mundo. It seemed as though the world was going to end. My sisters and I were scared.

It was pitch darkness when loud crying began. It was midnight when everyone had to help with very loud noises that meant Our Lord had died. Beating on Penitente drums and the whirling of matracas could be heard. There were also piercing sounds from flutes. The hard pounding of whips on the backs of the Hermanos de Sangre, the brothers of blood, were unbearable. Added to everything were the clanging of chains and the scraping of washboards. I heard cloth being torn by people near me. Anything and everything that could make noises added to the confusion. After what seemed like an eternity, a Hermano de la Luz, a brother of light, lit the Candle of Christ. Our Savior resurrected, and there was peace.

Penitente Brotherhood matracas. Wood rattles have been used for generations on Good Friday to proclaim Christ's death on the cross.

An abandoned New Mexico morada, a meeting place of worship for the Penitente Brotherhood. *Photo by Lucia Dolores de Aragón.*

In her book *Trader on the Santa Fe Trail: The Memoirs of Franz Huning* (her grandfather), Lina Fergusson Browne wrote:

> *Penitente hunting in my youth was one of the recognized diversions at Easter time. To see this gruesome but fascinating sight we drove from Albuquerque to one of the villages rumored to be planning a celebration of the rites. These might differ as to size and in some details. Basically they consisted of a procession of men—six or eight, as many as thirty—stripped to the waist and wearing only white trousers. Every few steps they would stop and swing heavy whips of braided yucca fibers over their shoulders, lacerating their backs until streams of blood ran down onto the white trousers. The pito, a wood flute, provided a weird and haunting accompaniment to the swish of the penitential whips. The procession moved slowly through the village....Their objective was the morada (a chapel) where in complete darkness, services called Las Tinieblas (meaning total darkness) were held to recall the crucifixion of Christ, the accompanying storm suggested by a deafening din produced by rattling chains and the banging of tin kettles and pans.*

I

WONDERS OF THE INVISIBLE WORLD

MAL OJO (EVIL EYE)

¡Nunca fijes la mirada, puedes hacer Mal Ojo!

Never stare, you could give Evil Eye!

It was one of those dark and gloomy days one would rather forget. Two funerals were taking place at the ancient San Juan Cemetery in the Spanish village of San Jose. One was for a man in his nineties. He was a gentleman who had lived a good life. This old one had been as strong as an ox, but as luck would have it, he tripped and banged his head. That was it. The other funeral, which was taking place about one hundred feet away, was for a much younger person. It was for a woman in her late sixties. This woman had gone through a very hard life. Like the saying goes, she had worked her fingers to the bone.

Juan Sánchez was the old man's nephew. They had been close, almost like father and son. Juan was a man in his forties. He was not very smart, but not ignorant either. There were things he just couldn't understand or deal with, like the passing of his parents when he was quite young. Now he led a humdrum life, but on this day, his life would be changed forever. There were few mourners for Juan's uncle. They came from a small family, but the other funeral had a large crowd. And the crying was unbearable. It was so loud it could have awakened the dead buried nearby. Juan couldn't help but notice what was going on at the other funeral. Although he had his own cross to bear, he was concerned. Suddenly, a middle-aged woman with gray hair left the crowd and ran to where he and his relatives stood. She was moving

Early nineteenth-century Mal Ojo silver talisman. Powerful magical and protective charms were worn around the neck. Variations of eye symbols helped combat "evil eye."

at such a fast pace she almost tripped. When she got to their gravesite, she yelled out, "Is there a Juan or a Juana here?" He reluctantly admitted his name was Juan and wondered why she asked. "Wait here," she begged. "I'll be right back." She returned moments later with a much younger woman who was holding a baby. The infant was crying hysterically. The voice of the older woman rang out, "¡Alguien le hizo Mal Ojo a Lupita, ayúdale por favor!" (Someone gave Lupita the evil eye, can you please help her?) "Help her how?" Juan asked. "What can I do for her?" "Cure her," the woman answered. "Please help her!"

In the past, and even in some isolated areas of New Mexico today, people believed in the mysterious powers of Mal Ojo (Evil Eye). The belief in the supernatural powers of the eyes arrived in New Mexico with the Spanish settlers in 1598. This tenet was ancient in Spain. No one knows the origins of this idea. What is known is the idea of the power in malevolent glares is as old as civilization itself. In fact, Greek philosophers Plato, Plutarch and other famous sages mention Evil Eye in their writings and believed in this power. Plutarch stated something to the effect that the eyes are the main source of the deadliest rays, which are supposed to rise up as poisoned arrows from the most inner recesses of humans when they give the Evil Eye to others. Ancient peoples thought fixed stares came from those who could enchant. The prows of ancient ships sometimes featured concentric blue-and-white balls or disks to ward off the strange powers of the Evil Eye.

In New Mexico, there is a prevalent thought that if people are especially attractive, beautiful or handsome, they are susceptible to harm from Evil

Eye. If it's an infant or a child, it's not unusual for someone to spit on a finger and make a sign of the cross on the forehead, thereby blessing them to ward off Mal Ojo. If Evil Eye is not prevented, the afflicted suffer from misfortune, serious injury and may even die from the maladies that are inflicted by this supernatural force. Someone can give Mal Ojo intentionally by wishing someone harm. Not all is lost though. Anyone named Juan or Juana can cure Evil Eye because they have powers provided by the forces of good against evil. This idea may have come from the belief that St. John the Baptist possessed powers ordinary men of his time did not have or understand. St. John baptized Jesus Christ, the Nazarene.

In many nations, there was a fascination with the eyes. Talismans were produced to protect people from those capable of inflicting this strength over them. Objects believed to have magical or protective powers included silver images of eyes called *milagros* (miracles). Amulets or charms used against evil or injury in New Mexico included something as simple as a clove of garlic. This was strung up and placed around the necks of infants or toddlers. How did people know when someone was possessed? If someone was afflicted, this person yawned profusely. If one placed olive oil in water and oil floated, then there was no Evil Eye. However, if the olive oil sank to the bottom, then it was present. If the oil separated when two or more drops were placed in water, then there was no problem. But if the drops merged and became larger, then Evil Eye had to be cured. The number of drops of olive oil that dissolved in water could determine the strength of Evil Eye. Wearing the color black could be useful. A raw chicken egg rolled over the body and then broken into a glass of water was considered a good test. The glass of water was placed under the bed and checked by morning. If the egg appeared cooked, the person had Evil Eye. Then it was believed that the affliction had transferred to the egg and the victim was cured.

The earliest known document in New Mexico mentioning Evil Eye dates to February 11, 1733. Albuquerque *alcalde* (mayor) Don Gonzales Blas accused Melcor Trujillo of inflicting Evil Eye on a man named Vicente García and his wife. Captain Agosto Rael and Lieutenant José Reano filed the original complaint. Both declared they were present in the García home when the incident occurred. Both husband and wife became extremely ill while under Melcor's spell. Melcor could have cured the poor souls, but according to the complaint, he chose not to do so.

Lieutenant Reano testified at trial he saw Melcor provide the victims with a drink. After this, both were bedridden. They appeared dead but suddenly revived. The awestruck lieutenant said no words could describe what happened. It turned out that Melcor had given the couple a drug called peyote. Indian medicine men used this in their religious ceremonies. Peyote comes from a small, spineless ribbed cactus that contains hallucinogens. During the lengthy proceeding, it was discovered that several individuals had been involved in a plot to hurt others. Some of the instigators were Indians, including the chief, from Isleta Pueblo. According to the testimony of a witness, idols had been used to cast spells.

Curanderas, women healers of New Mexico who treated illnesses with medicinal herbs, recited a certain prayer to help protect against Evil Eye. They said, "Holy Mother [In reference to Mary, the mother of Christ], Our Lady of Light, if Florencia [name is used as an example], is suffering from Mal Ojo, Evil Eye, please pray for her, guide her, protect her and release her." This was repeated three times. But this was not all. Certain plants and roots were believed to have great powers. In the past—and the present, in some cases—Native Americans believed witches possessed the ability to call on the supernatural to cast evil spells. This could be done not only with chants but also with the use of certain ingredients. What could be done to relieve this pain and suffering? *Curanderos* (witch doctors) in Mexico practiced what was known as the "dark arts." They treated patients by calling on supernatural spirits in many ways. Curanderas in New Mexico—who were distinctly separate from their Mexican counterparts—maintained that the Roman Catholic faith and religion played an extremely important part in the treatment of disease and illness, whether physical or emotional.

The belief in protective personal angels, saints that one was named after and the most Blessed Mother of Christ, and El Padre Jesús Nazareno, Jesus Christ himself, was crucial to one's wellbeing. Since New Mexicans were descended from early Spanish colonists who had memories of the horrible pandemics in Europe, some of the Spanish beliefs and superstitions were indeed transplanted in New Mexico. Cures included plants and roots. For example, *barba de maíz* (corn silk) was used by Indian medicine men and Hispanic New Mexican curanderas in healings for generations. The root of *cachaña* (blazing star, *Liatris punctata*, snakeroot), also called gray feather root, was halved, and a cross was carved in one half to be worn around the neck. It was placed on the body to ward off any kind of curse or evil spell. Cachaña roots were believed to be especially successful in protection against Evil Eye. It was a sacred protection cast against those who principally admired a very beautiful girl, or boy. Those casting Evil Eye could possibly take them, and for, whatever reason, the ones cursed would never be released, or seen again.

Osha was the best-known plant in New Mexico along with manzanilla (chamomile). The principal qualities of the medicinal osha root were passed down from one culture to another. The roots were boiled to combat viral illnesses and several other ailments. The tea is calming and works well against flu-like symptoms. Osha was used during the great influenza epidemic that took many lives in New Mexico around 1918. Other plants such as yerba buena (spearmint) and plumajillo (yarrow) were also used. Osha was and is believed to do well in dealing with witchcraft curses, and evil spirits. Of course, a garlic clove worn around the neck on a string, or chain, was protection against all evil. Garlic was once thought to ward off vampires. In New Mexico, garlic and onions were believed to hold many healthful properties.

2

BOLAS DE LUMBRE
(ORBS OF FIRE)

An all-night vigil was being held at the Santuario de Chimayo near Española. This famous religious sanctuary was built around 1819. It is said the Spanish Colonial–style mission church has a miraculous hole of sacred soil that never empties, no matter how much of the dirt is removed. This soil is said to cure illnesses. Many crippled pilgrims claimed they were cured completely at the Santuario when medical science could do nothing for them. These devoted faithful left crutches hung on the walls to prove it. This Catholic holy site and shrine is located thirty-eight miles north of Santa Fe on New Mexico State Highway 76. The ailing, the weak, the religious and the curious come here. Contact with the earth cures those who are in need of physical and spiritual help. The devout also venerate a special image of El Santo Niño de Atocha (the Holy Child of Atocha) here. According to legend, Spanish knights were being held in a prison by the Moorish in Atocha, Spain, around the twelfth century. These poor soldiers were dying from thirst and hunger. One day, a young boy carrying a basket of bread and a gourd filled with water appeared. Since he was a child, the Moors let him into the prison. He gave the prisoners bread and water, saving them. The bread did not run out, and neither did the water. People believed it was the Christ child who had appeared.

At the Santuario, a wood image of the Holy Child produced by an early santero was venerated. Miracles were attributed to this figure. For example, they said the image would become animated at night, traveling around the countryside and performing acts of mercy and miracles for those in

Above: The world-famous Chimayo Church. Ink and watercolor by Miro K. Thousands of pilgrims visit this holy place with its miraculous soil.

Left: Santo Niño de Atocha is a very popular religious image in New Mexico. People claim the animated figure of the Christ child performs miracles at night.

Nineteenth-century engravings portraying strange luminous fireballs seen in buildings. This one entered through the chimney, swirled around and left in 1886.

desperate need. The Holy Child would wear out his shoes while doing these wonderful deeds and then return to the Santuario when he was done. His worn-out shoes were replaced every year.

Lucia Dolores accompanied her family on their annual pilgrimage. During the devotional preparation for the Christmas season, the small church was filled to capacity. People were even standing on the sides and in the back. Lit candles flickered on the walls, casting mysterious shadows from the wooden santos. There was a loud thunderstorm outside and flashing lightning. Everyone was completely silent when the large wooden doors at the entrance were blown open. Suddenly, a luminous sphere the size of a basketball flew in. It traveled up the aisle and whirled around near the altar. Hearts were frozen as the silent glowing ball stood stationary and then just as suddenly flew back out the doorway. Pandemonium followed in the Santuario.

It is estimated that only 3 percent of the world's population has experienced these strange orbs of fire or light. On December 24, 1726,

Dr. Johann Faust sees a luminous glowing object. People called these mysterious spheres "magic disks." *Engraving by Rembrandt Van Rijn, 1652. Public domain.*

the *London Journal* reported a sighting on the sloop *Catherine and Mary*. John Howell, who was on board, stated, "As we were coming thro' the Gulf of Florida on the 29th of August, 1726, when a large ball of fire fell from the *Element* [name of ship] and split our mast in Ten Thousand Pieces, if it were possible; split our main Beam, also three planks of the side, Under Water, and Three of the Deck."

Howell claimed one man died and another was injured during this terrifying experience. During another occurrence that took place at a church in England, it was said an eight-foot ball of fire nearly destroyed the building before flying out a window, leaving a large hole. Churchgoers described the fearful object as "God's Wrath" and the "Flames of Hell." Eyewitnesses elsewhere said, "This delegation from the clouds at times played tag for half an hour and then vanished into thin air."

Round luminous objects that appear quickly and without warning have been reported for centuries in New Mexico and around the world. Accounts have described these orbs as perplexing, weird and sometimes deadly. Scientists have used terms such as *globe lightning*, *lightning balls* and *ball lightning* to describe these phenomena, which have an unknown origin. Sightings of these lighted spheres rank with UFOs and defy a complete explanation for their appearances. They have been described as pea-sized to several meters in diameter. A handful of reports say the balls eventually explode, leaving behind an odor of sulfur, a pale yellow natural nonmetallic element. These thought-provoking forms stimulate our need to know more, so scientists have offered hypotheses about their existence. What is known is these unusual aerial phenomena are infrequent, unpredictable and move horizontally. Sometimes larger spheres split into smaller ones. They may also be the source of some ancient New Mexico legends.

During World War II, pilots reported fast-moving, small, round, glowing objects that followed their aircraft. These made wild and rapid turns and changed direction before they disappeared. The balls of light appeared so often and traveled in such strange trajectories that American pilots called them "foo fighters." They couldn't be outmaneuvered and appeared to be under some intelligent control. They were called "Kraut Fireballs" in Europe. It was generally believed these were secret German weapons being produced in Hitler's labs. After the war was over, it was discovered that German scientists were working on a saucer-shaped flying object similar to those that continue to remain unidentified up to the present day.

Román Jaramillo relating his experiences as a sheepherder during the 1920s. He often saw luminous orbs, spirits and strange things late at night on the range.

Bola de Lumbre. A witch in fire stretches her hand and fingers out. *Photo by Lucia Dolores de Aragón.*

Modern-day scientists have attempted to recreate glowing spheres in labs but continue to be unsuccessful in recreating those that have been seen. The bolas de lumbre continue to evade legitimate scientific study and analysis. They are still seen in New Mexico, where people say they lead one to hidden treasure or are witches who can transform themselves into balls of fire and dance at night.

3

RAISING THE DEAD

De la suerte y la muerte no hay nadie que se escape.

From luck and death there is no one that escapes.

There is a darker side to history about raising the dead that was introduced into New Mexico. For example, in the fourteenth century, a young man named Pedro, the son of King Afonso IV of Portugal, fell madly in love. His love interest was the hapless Inês Piras de Castro. She was of noble blood, but King Afonso felt this young woman was unsuitable for his pampered son. He was determined to separate the two lovebirds no matter what the cost. Poor unfortunate Pedro still wanted to marry Inês. In January 1355, King Afonso had Inês murdered to get her permanently out of the way. Four years later, Afonso died, and Pedro ascended to the throne of Portugal. King Pedro had his true love exhumed from the grave. As luck would have it, her body was incorruptible. The new king had Inês crowned queen and placed on a throne next to his. Nobles had to lift her hand and kiss it to demonstrate their fealty. Some of the nobility even had to pay a fee for this most unusual honor. The king repaid their kindness not only with his gratitude but also with royal acts of enrichment. Some of the nobles were astonished and very pleased. They were then quite willing to pay for the privilege of honoring the dead Inês. The royal court was fascinated and drawn to the strange actions of the peculiar king.

Interestingly, some the early settlers of New Mexico were from Portugal. Although the Portuguese did not directly influence Spanish culture, bizarre and unusual beliefs and practices from the Middle Ages filtered into Spain from additional areas of Europe. Odd customs were obviously introduced into the territory when trade between New Mexico and the United States opened up with the Santa Fe Trail in the early nineteenth century. This became especially prevalent after 1846, when New Mexico was taken over by the United States during the Mexican-American War. By this time, a number of New Mexicans knew how to read and write in both Spanish and English. American soldiers, merchants, traders and ordinary citizens carried along their reading material. This included a popular periodical called the *Anglo American* and what would become known as penny dreadfuls.

The cheap serial literature, also called penny horribles or bloods, appeared in New Mexico. They were first published in the 1830s. Some issues centered on supernatural entities.

On Saturday, May 8, 1847, A.D. Paterson, the editor of the *Anglo American* in New York, posted a section that received a great deal of attention and prompted a series titled "Letters on the Truths Contained in Popular Superstitions." He included the following sensational story about a village that was located near the capital city of Belgrade, Yugoslavia, during the eighteenth century.

> *It was in the spring of 1727 that there returned from the Levant to the village of Meduegna, near Belgrade, one Arnod Paole, who, in a few years of military service and varied adventure, had amassed enough to purchase him a cottage, and an acre or two of land in his native place....One day...Arnod missed his footing and fell from the top of his hay wagon. He was picked up stunned and insensible. They carried him home; where, lingering some hours, he died; was buried....Several in the neighborhood made complaints that they had been haunted by the deceased Arnod; and four of the number died....The villagers were advised by their Heyduke... to disinter the body of Arnod Paole....The body was found in a perfectly fresh state, with no signs of decomposition. Fresh blood had recently escaped from its mouth, with which its shirt was wet. The skin had separated with the nails, and there were new skin and nails underneath. As it was perfectly clear from these signs that it was a vampyr, conformably to the use established in such cases, they drove a stake through his heart.*

THE ANGLO AMERICAN.

A. D. PATERSON,
EDITOR.

E. L. GARVIN & Co.
PUBLISHERS.

FOUR DOLLARS A YEAR | "AUDI ALTERAM PARTEM." | PAYABLE IN ADVANCE

OFFICE } 4 Barclay-St. Astor Building | **NEW YORK, SATURDAY, MAY 8, 1847.** | VOL. 9, No. 3.

APRIL.

April has come—with her silver dew,
And the shout in her woods of the lone cuckoo ;
Heard by us all—as we lock on a star—
Ever in fondness, but ever afar ;
Luring the boy, as he loiters from school,
Through the long fields, like an April day's fool ;
Wiling the lover, as though it were Love,
O'er the green meadow and through the dim grove ;
Shouting like hope, till we follow its strain,
Then hiding, like joy, in the forest again ;
Heard in each tree, though on none of them seen,
Making us sad amid sunlight and green !
But the morals of April are taught us too soon,—
The heart and the cuckoo as yet are in tune ;
For the *sadness* is sweet in the Spring of the year,—
And we find not the grief till the forest be sere.
Lover and boy will not see what they should,
But practise through life what they learnt in the wood :—
All that eludes them still fain to pursue,
And hunt through the world for the flying cuckoo !

April has come ! — the capricious in mien—
With her wreath of the rainbow and sandals of green ;
Storms on her forehead, and flowers at her feet,
And many toned voices—but all of them sweet ;
Clouding the heaven, but scenting the glade—
Weaving with brightness and warping with shade !
Dampness her carpet and dimness her roof,
But threads of the sunbeam shot through their woof ;
Playing, like childhood, with tear and with smile,—
Weeping for ever, and laughing the while !
Like a beautiful witch in the woodland she dwells,
Muttering magic and playing with spells :
Mixing her charms over meadows and bowers,
Throwing her seeds in and taking out flowers ;
Nursing the blooms —that she scents but fade,
For the passeth away ere a bud has decayed !
Oh ! many a wreath for her sisters she weaves,
And builds them up houses of blossoms and leaves,—
Months follow, fairer, when April is gone,
But none of the year hath a gift like her own.—
Richer their colors and sweeter their breath,
But no month of the year all sees so little of DEATH.

And yet through her cycle the year is the same,
And death in the field but a symbol and name ;—
For Nature knows nought—like the heart—of a frost
In which flower shall be withered and *seed* shall be lost,—
When hope—like its object is swallowed in gloom,
And the green—with the blossom—goes down to the tomb.
And April—the weeper—yet knows not the tear
That can never be dried since no sunshine is near,
Nor smile—the mortal—that looks from the eye
More sadly than tears—when *their* fountain is dry !
Her darkest of gifts is the shadow she throws,
To soften her light—wile it nurtures the rose !
And her best, what she leaves as she passes away,
In her tents of the flower TO BE FOLLOWED BY MAY !

T. K. HERVEY.

LETTERS ON THE TRUTHS CONTAINED
IN POPULAR SUPERSTITIONS.
II.—VAMPYRISM.

Dear Archy,—In acknowledging my former letter, you express an eager desire to learn, as you phrase it, "all about vampyrs, if there ever were such things." I will not delay satisfying your curiosity, wondering only how my friend, your late tutor, Mr. H., should have left you in a state of uncertainty upon a point on which, in my time, schoolboys many years your juniors had fully made up their minds.

"Were there ever such things as vampyrs !" *tamtamne rem tam negligenter ?* I turn to the learned pages of Horst for a luminous and precise definition of the destructive and mysterious beings, whose existence you have ventured to consider problematical.

"A vampyr is a dead body, which continues to live in the grave, which it leaves, however, by night, for the purpose of sucking the blood of the living, whereby it is nourished, and preserved in good condition, instead of becoming decomposed like other dead bodies."

Upon my word you really deserve—since Mr. George Combe has clearly shown in his admirable work "On the Constitution of Man, and its adaptation to the world around him," that ignorance is a statutable crime before Nature, and punishable, and punished by the laws of Providence,—you deserve, I say, unless you contrive to make Mr. H. your substitute, which I think would be just, yourself to be the subject of the nocturnal visit of a vampyr. Your scepticism will abate pretty considerably, when you see him stealthily entering your room, yet are powerless under the fascination of his fixed and leaden eye—when you are conscious, as you lie motionless with terror, of his nearer and nearer approach,—when you feel his face, fresh with the smell of the grave,

bent over your throat, while his keen teeth make a fine incision in your jugular, preparatorily to his commencing his plain, but nutritive repast.

You would look a little paler the next morning, but that would be all for the moment ; for Fischer informs us that the bite of a vampyr leaves in general no mark upon the person. But he fearfully adds. " it (the bite) is nevertheless speedily fatal, unless the bitten person protect himself by eating some of the earth from the grave of the vampyr, and smearing himself with his blood." Unfortunately, indeed, these measures are only of temporary use. Fischer adds, " it through these precautions the life of the victim be prolonged for a period, sooner or later he ends with becoming a vampyr himself ; that is to say, he dies, and is buried, but continues to lead a vampyr life in the grave, nourishing himself by infecting others, and promiscuously propagating vampyrism."

Now this is no romancer's dream. It is a succinct account of a superstition, which to this day survives in the east of Europe, where little more than a century ago it was frightfully prevalent. At that epoch, vampyrism spread like an epidemic pestilence through Servia and Wallachia, causing innumerable deaths, and disturbing all the land with apprehension of the mysterious visitation, against which no one felt his life secure.

This is something like a good solid practical popular delusion. Do I believe it !—to be sure I do ; the facts are matter of history. The people died like sheep, and the cause and method of their dying was, in their belief, what has just been stated. You suppose, then, they died, frightened out of their lives ; as men have died, whose pardon has been proclaimed when their necks were already on the block, of the belief they were going to die ! Well, if that were all, the subject would be worth examining : but there is more in it than that, as the following o'er true tale will convince you, the essential parts of which are attested by perfect documentary evidence.

It was in the spring of 1727 that there returned from the Levant to the village of Meduegna, near Belgrade, one Arnod Paole, who, in a few years of military service and varied adventure, had amassed enough to purchase him a cottage, and an acre or two of land in his native place, where he gave out he meant to pass the remainder of his days. He kept his word. Arnod had yet scarcely reached the prime of manhood ; and though he must have encountered the rough, as well as the smooth of life, and have mingled with many a wild and reckless companion, yet his natural good disposition, and honest principle, had preserved him unscathed amid the scenes he had passed through. At all events, such were the thoughts expressed by the neighbours, as they discussed his return among them in the stube of the village Hof. Nor did the frank and open countenance of Arnod, his obliging habits, and steady conduct, argue their judgment incorrect. Nevertheless, there was something occasionally noticeable in his ways, a look and tone that betrayed inward inquietude. Often would he refuse to join his friends, or on some sudden plea abruptly quit their society. And he still more unaccountably, and as it seemed systematically, avoided meeting his pretty neighbour, Nina, whose father occupied the next tenement to his own. At the age of seventeen, Nina was as charming a picture as you could have seen, of youth, cheerfulness, innocence, and confidence in all the world. You could not look into her limpid eyes, which steadily returned your gaze, without seeing to the bottom of the pure and transparent spring of her thoughts. Then why did Arnod shrink from meeting her ! He was young, had a little property, had health and industry, and he had told his friends he had formed no ties in other lands Why, then, did he avoid the fascination of the pretty Nina, who seemed a being made to chase from any brow the clouds of gathering care ? But he did so. Yet less and less resolutely ; for he felt the charm of her presence ; who could have done otherwise ? and how could he at last resist—he didn't—the impulse of his fondness for the innocent girl who often sought to cheer his fits of depression ?

And they were to be united ; were betrothed ; yet still an anxious gloom would fitfully overcast his countenance even in the sunshine of those hours.

" What is it, dear Arnod, that makes you sad ? it cannot be on my account, I know ; for you were sad before you ever noticed me ; and that I think," and you should have seen the deepening rose upon her cheek, as she added, " surely first made me notice you."

" Nina," he answered, " I have done, I fear, a great wrong in trying to gain your affections. Nina, I have a fixed impression that I shall not live ; yet, know ag this, I have selfishly made my existence necessary to your happiness."

" How strangely you talk, dear Arnod ! Who in the village is stronger and healthier than you ! You feared no danger when you were a soldier ; what danger do you fear as a villager of Meduegna ?"

" It haunts me, Nina "—

" But, Arnod, you were sad before you thought of loving me. Did you then fear to die ?"

" Ah, Nina, it is something worse than death :" and his vigorous frame shook with agony.

" Arn d, I conjure you, tell me."

" It was in Cossova this fate befel me. Here we have hitherto escaped the terrible scourge. But there they died, and the dead visited the living. I experienced a first frightful visitation, and I fled, but not till I had sought his grave, and exacted the dread expiation from the vampyr."

Nina uttered a piercing cry, and fell senseless. Afterwards, they found a consolation in the length of time, now months, that had elapsed, since Arnod had left Cossova, during which no fearful visitant had again approached him ; and they fondly began to hope *that* gave them security. For the poor girl knew from many a village tale the danger to which Arnod had been exposed.

It is a strange world. The ills we fear often never befall us : the blows th reach us are for the most part unforeseen ones. One day, about a week after this conversation, Arnod missed his footing and fell from the top of his hay

The writer went on to say that attempts to eradicate a potential epidemic of vampirism in the village were unsuccessful. Gravediggers worked from sunup to sundown, exhuming and reburying for several days. The *Anglo American* writer commented:

> *The document which gives these particulars is signed by three regimental surgeons, and formally countersigned by the lieutenant-colonel and a sub-lieutenant; it appears the date of June 7, 1732, Meduegna, near Belgrade, no less so, that it does not stand alone, but is supported by heaps of parallel evidence, only less rigorously verifiable. It appears to me to establish beyond a question, that, where the fear and belief of vampyrism is prevailing, and there occur several deaths after short illness, the bodies, when disinterred, after weeks after burial, present corpses, from which life has only recently departed. . . . What inference shall we draw from this fact?—that vampirism is true in the popular sense and that these fresh looking and well-conditioned corpses had some mysterious way of preternaturally nourishing themselves?*

The belief systems of both Native Americans and those of Spanish descent in New Mexico revolved around spirituality and the animate force of the soul in contrast to the dead returning to life to nourish themselves. Some Americans thought that anything and everything could be bought and sold, including the dead.

Certain Native American tribes were not concerned about the dead rising up from graves. They were preoccupied with ghosts or spirits that returned. Bodies were taken as far away from the villages as possible. Burial parties took loved ones into the hills or nearby mountains. They placed the bodies into crevices and covered them up with brush, dirt and rocks. Personal belongings were either broken or placed with the dead. The burial group, which numbered as few as three or four, then returned home. They would travel by a different route and would never look back. This was considered bad luck and could mean whoever looked back would be next to die. At the village, mourners burned pungent plants such as juniper and sage as "ghost medicine." They would bathe with the smoke. The plant ashes would then be spread around everywhere to discourage the dead person's spirit from returning and from staying to haunt the living. Everything that the deceased had possessed was destroyed. Not even the names of those who had passed away could be spoken. Nomadic Indians believed that the ghosts of the dead could be inclined to return to their homes, so encampments were moved to deter this from happening.

New Mexico Hispanic villagers also believed in spirits. When someone died, they produced their own coffins, which were often made from pine and cottonwood crude lumber. The hand-hewn coffins were placed on tables in the largest rooms of the house. They were then covered with gray muslin, and black crosses were lovingly placed on the lids. Containers with sliced onions or pungent plants were placed under the pine wood tables to diminish odors. Caskets were then surrounded with slender lit candles. All of the mirrors were covered or were turned toward the wall. Some would say that if anyone looked into a mirror, he or she would be the next to die.

All of the women wore long, fringed black shawls. Those entering into the house knelt and prayed for the welfare of the soul and its repose, "Que descanse el alma de [nombre] en paz." (May the soul of [name] rest in peace). During the wake, Penitente watchers prayed mournful funeral hymns. After this, those who gathered discussed the last moments of the deceased in detail. The chanting of *alabados*, religious hymns, was interspersed with wailing. The rosary was prayed at midnight. The next day, a procession took the casket for burial. The mourners stopped at designated rest stops called *descansos*, placed the casket down and prayed the rosary and other prayers for the soul of the deceased. At the gravesite, a lengthy time was spent on prayers and meditation. Death was both a family and a community affair that cost nothing but hard work and caring, which were both sacred and vital to the living.

In contrast, death was highly commercialized in the United Sates in the nineteenth century. There were no funeral homes in New Mexico at the time Americans took over the territory. After newly arrived Americans died, they were placed in storerooms. General merchants were in charge of all funeral arrangements, including purchasing caskets and hiring gravediggers. Once undertakers or morticians set up shop in New Mexico, funeral parlors were then available. The shady practices of the American funeral industry began to slowly take over. Lavishly upholstered coffins manufactured with specialty woods or with intricately embossed metals were shipped into New Mexico. These were readily available in the east. Cosmetic "reconstruction" of faces became a fine art. Cheeks were puffed up with cotton or fabric. Different makeup was used to "dress things up," with faces that often looked ghoulish. Bodies were embalmed with snake oils or alcohol. Caskets holding bodies were then placed into tranquil "slumber rooms." Friends and family could see them there. Needless to say, the deceased looked nothing like themselves. In fact, they were virtually unrecognizable after American morticians took over. The dead were embellished before burial. Later, laws were passed that prohibited burial traditions in New Mexico. Special mourning clothing for women and children was sold. Photographers took photos of the dead and sold these as mementos. Families of those who had passed away were convinced by photographers that they needed these extremely unconventional images for their photo albums and memories. Postmortem photographers posed the living around the coffin. They also had dead children seated on chairs. Mothers were shown sitting with their dead young. Others held dead infants in their arms. Rosy tints on images added to the morbid flavor of the pictures. American death souvenirs in this bizarre trade included braided hair relics of the deceased encased in gold lockets and other jewelry. Hair was also placed into elaborate boxed frames and many other pricy memento mori objects. Death was an American commodity meant to be fully profitable, and the practices spread along the Santa Fe Trail when New Mexico was taken over.

Americans attempted to remove all vestiges of Indian religions in New Mexico and made it a crime if they practiced their sacred rituals. This included native death practices. They were to be Americanized. Morticians and death for profit with elaborately manufactured coffins and lavish tombstones gradually replaced the family affairs. This paved the way for unorthodox burial methods in New Mexico, such as mausoleums, and large stately tombs. In order to avoid premature burials, funeral parlors offered coffins with springs and latches for the deceased to use just in case they revived. Bells and other contraptions were also available for those who were laid to rest in the mausoleums. This way those prematurely interred could announce they were still alive, thereby returning from the dead. But the most forbidden American custom of commercializing the dead was selling bodies for profit.

Around 1841, the medical department at St. Louis University in Missouri was established. According to the historical record, a building housing this department, or college, was located on Washington Avenue. The medical faculty included individuals from North Carolina, Kentucky, Alabama, Indiana and other areas. Among these men were Dr. M.L. Linton and Dr. William Carr Lane. The department was an immediate success. Richard Edwards wrote, "It is an ornament to the city, and is a splendid offering to the elevating purposes of progressive science." There were countless eager students desiring to be educated in the medical sciences of the time. They were also anxious to begin their individual practices.

In the United States, Dr. M.L. Linton was considered an eminent physician. He was born in Nelson County, Kentucky, on April 12, 1808. It is written that

Body snatchers digging up a body. Stealing corpses for medical schools became a lucrative business in the United States. *Drawing from* A Tour of St. Louis *by James W. Buel and Joseph A. Dacus, 1878.*

he read medical books as a young boy and was determined to pursue medicine as a career. He studied under Dr. J.H. Polin in Springfield, Massachusetts. Linton eventually graduated from Transylvania College in Lexington, Kentucky. After that he spent some time studying oversees in Europe, Dr. Linton published the *St. Louis Medical Journal* in 1843. He wrote *Outlines of Pathology, the Manifestations of Disease in the Anatomy* as a textbook for his students. Dr. Linton became president of the Medical Society of St. Louis.

Dr. William Carr Lane was born on December 1, 1789, in Fayette County, Pennsylvania. He studied under Drs. Collins and Johnson in Louisville, Kentucky. Lane enlisted in Colonel Russell's Brigade, commanded by Major Zachary Taylor, to fight the Northwest Indians in 1813. General Taylor was renowned as a hero during the Mexican-American War. When Missouri became a state, Lane was appointed as the first quartermaster general. He became the first mayor of St. Louis when it was incorporated as a city and served as mayor for nine years. Dr. Lane also served for three years in the Missouri legislature. He had a professor's chair in the medical department of Kemper's College. President Millard Fillmore appointed Dr. William Carr Lane governor of the territory of New Mexico in 1852. Lane and Linton were not only contemporaries but also of the same mind when it came to New Mexico.

Left: Dr. M.L. Linton established the *St. Louis Medical Journal* in 1843. As president of the Medical Society of St. Louis he promoted buying illicit corpses for medical studies.

Right: Dr. William Carr Lane led the training of medical students with cadavers in Missouri. President Millard Fillmore appointed Lane territorial governor of New Mexico in 1852.

Missouri Medical College (*left*) next to a religious academy in St. Louis. Missouri medical schools led the nation in the purchase of illicit bodies for studies.

The lucrative trade between Santa Fe and Missouri and the rest of the United States introduced many American individuals and families seeking a new way of life in prosperous New Mexico Territory. Unfortunately, land thieves, crooked lawyers, con men, snake oil peddlers, Confederate bandits and other nefarious and criminal people also streamed in along with well-meaning immigrants. The most despicable of all of the new arrivals were the "Resurrectionists."

The macabre practices of body snatchers known as Resurrectionists in Missouri and other parts of the country included the stealing of valuables that were buried with the bodies. Objects of value that were stolen from burials included gold rings, silver and gold necklaces, bracelets and pendants. Anything that could be sold, pawned and traded was taken. This included artifacts from Native American burials such as clay pots and leather goods. Early American merchants and traders in Santa Fe built up very profitable businesses with the purchase of stolen burial objects. Tomb robbing and plundering spread throughout the country and was introduced into New Mexico with the opening of the Santa Fe Trail.

It is estimated that medical schools in Missouri needed five hundred cadavers annually. Dead bodies were essential for dissection and the study of anatomy. The correct practice of civility with bodies of the deceased was to provide medical studies legally with unclaimed bodies, unidentified persons or those who bequeathed their remains. Other cadavers studied were those of people who died through accident, murder, suicide or illness. Those who died from certain ailments were especially in demand because it was felt doctors needed to determine what caused their deaths. A trade in corpses was set during this era of body snatchers who sold the dead to doctors at medical schools. Doctors who had no integrity asked no questions and paid high prices.

It is ironic that some grave robbers in Missouri were the medical students themselves. Ghoulish merchants of remains sometimes hid pickled bodies in barrels and shipped these by train or freight wagon to medical schools in Missouri from other areas. A substantial amount of money could be made—as high as twenty-five or thirty dollars for each body, depending on the need. This was a considerable amount for the times. A great deal of land and yearly provisions could be purchased with the sale of one corpse. So this was quite a lucrative business. After Indian battles, or massacres, for example, many of the dead bodies were picked up and sold to medical schools. Resurrectionists sold the bodies of Indians that were hanged or those sentenced to execution. It is difficult to trace public cases since grave robbery became such a common practice. On February 7, 1891, the *Daily Citizen* of Albuquerque, New Mexico, reported some interesting items in its "Town Talk" section:

> *J.W. Westmorland, a native of St. Louis, Mo. Died at the residence of Mr. Lane, colored, early this morning. He arrived here last October, and after a short stay, left for Winslow. He returned to the city several weeks ago and secured a room at Mr. Lane's, where he died. He was a victim of consumption. The deceased was a member of the colored lodges of Masons and Odd Fellows of St. Louis, and his body will be embalmed by Mr. Kremple and shipped east tomorrow....C.W. Lewis and W.L. Trimble started this morning to dig for the supposed hidden money of old man Antonio Sandoval, long since dead. The land on which the money is supposed to have been buried surrounds the old church at Barelas....It is claimed that at least $600,000 were deposited in the ground....The handsomest hearse that has ever been seen in New Mexico will soon be found at the stable of Andy Horne, and it will run to the cemeteries at reasonable prices.*

The altars of the massive churches built during the Spanish colonial period included burials of the dead in the floors. In time, the deceased were buried outside, in front and on the sides of churches in areas considered to be consecrated or holy ground. This practice continued well into the American territorial period. Families also buried members on their private lands. With the gradual increase in population, public cemeteries were established. In the *Daily Citizen* notice it is interesting to find that Lewis and Trimble apparently used the excuse of digging for buried loot on the grounds of the Catholic church of Nuestro Sagrado Corazón, the Sacred Heart Church, in the old Spanish community of Barelas, near Albuquerque, in 1891. Some of the descendants of the original Spanish settlers started erecting wood fences with points and locked gates around burial plots. Wrought-iron fences encircling family burials were also used. Heavy rocks were piled over burials in some instances. Some people went so far as to pour concrete over the graves. According to a story titled "The Grave Robbers" carried by the *New York Times* on May 31, 1878, unethical behavior and dirty tricks were used in this black market trade in the United States. Resurrectionists hired mourners to claim bodies at morgues. A story is told in New Mexico that just before a burial, a mourner placed an object that was dear to the deceased near the feet, in a hidden area. When

Gravesite photo by Santiago Pacheco. During the late nineteenth-century, New Mexicans began piling heavy rocks on graves to deter Resurrectionists.

this person saw a similar coffin a year later at another funeral, he stuck his hand in and found the object.

The most notorious body snatcher in New Mexico may have been Dr. William Reuben Tipton, who was born on October 23, 1854, in Missouri. William and his parents settled in Watrous, New Mexico, in 1860, when he was six years old. Not much is known as to his early life, medical studies and early career. What is known about Tipton is that he was eventually named medical superintendent of the New Mexico Insane Asylum, a custodial or detention center situated at Las Vegas, New Mexico, now called the New Mexico State Hospital. The asylum, built in 1892, housed people with deformities and emotional and mental health problems. The majority of the patients were of Hispanic origin. It was not unusual for those with special needs, orphans or those who were rejected by society to be confined in asylums. Those institutions were notorious for the abuse of patients, as well as for unorthodox and pain-filled treatments akin to torture. Doctor Tipton was a skelologist, someone who scraped dead bodies to get to the skeletons.

Left: *Las Dolientes* (*The Mourners*), by Ray John de Aragón. Women criers were hired by grave robbers in New Mexico to feign a connection to unclaimed bodies.

Right: Dr. William Reuben Tipton from Missouri, superintendent of the New Mexico Insane Asylum. Tales of horror included finding scattered human bones. Corpses were for study.

New Mexico Territorial Asylum for the mentally impaired and handicapped, established in 1893. Horror stories abounded at the asylum, including studies of the dead.

A famous body-snatching story in New Mexico involved the remains of the notorious William H. Bonney, "Billy the Kid." After the Kid was shot on July 14, 1881, his body was buried at Fort Sumner, New Mexico. Russell Kistler, editor of the *Optic*, reported that five days after the burial, a "fearless skelologist" and an accomplice dug up the body. The remains, according to Kistler, were then transported to the office of a Las Vegas doctor who removed the head to secure the skull. The story goes that this unnamed doctor intended to reattach the skull to the skeleton. Another story relates that the flesh was removed from the Kid's entire body. It was not unusual during the nineteenth century for the bodies of celebrated or noted individuals to be stolen. In 1903, Dr. Tipton, the San Miguel County skelologist, was involved in a sensational scandal. According to the *Advertiser*, a local newspaper in Las Vegas, human bones had been found scattered about the grounds of the New Mexico Insane Asylum. Some employees at the asylum accused Dr. Tipton of the mistreatment of patients. After this was reported, territorial governor Miguel Antonio Otero ordered an investigation.

Historian Lynn Irwin Perrigo, PhD, wrote in his book *Gateway to Glorieta: A History of Las Vegas, New Mexico*,

> *Dr. Tipton admitted that when a patient without relatives had died, he had first performed an autopsy and next had scraped the flesh from the bones in order to have a skeleton for study. Hints were forthcoming that a young, insubordinate physician on the staff had purposely scattered those bones on the grounds in an effort to get Dr. Tipton removed.*

Dr. William Reuben Tipton was exonerated of all charges by the asylum board. This board was headed by Judge Elisha V. Long, a member of the notorious Santa Fe Ring—a group of corrupt judges, lawyers, politicians, officials, cattle and land thieves that operated in New Mexico beginning in the 1870s. Dr. Tipton died on August 25, 1924. By this time, the sprawling institution housed five hundred inmates that included both men and women.

I once read a *Ripley's Believe It or Not!* segment in a Sunday newspaper. Two men decided to burglarize a funeral home, but they had a difficult time removing the diamond wedding rings from one corpse. As the burglars were tugging and pulling, the deceased woman stood up. Both of them suffered strokes and died instantly. Unfortunately, there are many stories about those who have been buried prematurely. This was before embalming came into practice. Fluids are now injected into bodies to replace bodily fluids, including blood, to ensure that the person is indeed dead. It is quite interesting that fears from the past influence the fears of today. The walking dead, ghosts of those who have passed and haunted dwellings are still widespread. Alarm caused by expectations of danger coming from the unseen in the darkness lingers on in our darkest dreams.

4

DARK SIDE OF THE MOON

Los males persiguen los rayos de la luna.

Bad things follow the rays of the moon.

There are many things we now take for granted that began as superstitions. Although there may be evidence that contradicts what is generally believed, the idea continues to persist from one generation to the next. An ancient dogma in Western history and culture is that a full moon is associated with love. Mankind has always been spellbound by the different phases of the moon. The quarter, half and full moon have been used to determine cycles and seasons since time immemorial. The time for planting was planned systematically by the moon. A full moon guided the way for people in the dark. In New Mexico folklore, there can be a wicked, sinister, gloomy, dismal and disastrous side to the moon as this early saying warns: "Se lo comió la luna." (The moon ate him.)

In Taos, Alicia was eight months pregnant. This would be the first child for her and her husband, Tomas. One can imagine there were many women, both relatives and friends, who were giving Alicia advice. One who constantly counseled the young mother-to-be was her Tía Fidencia. Her elderly aunt would admonish her, "Tienes que tener mucho cuidado, niña." ("You have to be very careful, child.") Then Fidencia would tell her niece about the moon, since the young woman loved looking up at it during the nighttime. "The changing cycles of a woman's body are bewitched by the moon," the

Left: *La Maluna, or Mala Luna* (*The Bad Moon*). Painting by Rosalinda Pacheco. Fear of the moon as an image like La Llorona, could lay in wait at night.

Below: *Purple Rain* by Rosa María Calles. Belief in the strange and mysterious impact of the moon on the earth, animals, and humans was prevalent in New Mexico.

wise old aunt cautioned. It is known the moon is linked to human periods of gestation. A full moon is connected with the ebb and flow of ocean tides. A halo around the moon means bad or inclement weather is coming up. The moon also affects animal behavior. But what Fidencia told her niece was astounding. She warned her about the dangers of looking up at the moon while waiting to give birth. What the old woman thought has been a New Mexico–Spanish conviction for centuries. It was warned that women could not cut their hair or nails during a crescent moon. Girls couldn't either because then their hair and nails wouldn't grow out right. It was believed the

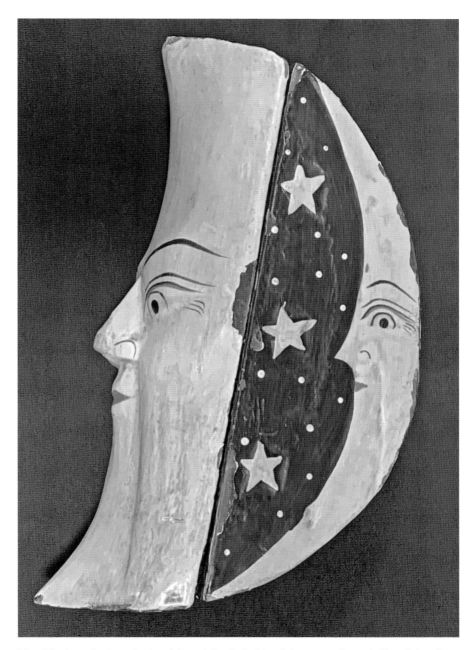

New Mexicans both praised and feared the dark side of the moon. It was believed that the moon controlled many human and animal emotions.

moon could cause deformities in the unborn. Did Alicia listen? She looked up at the full moon from the window in the hospital maternity ward anyway. She could have tied a set of keys around her waist as her aunt had told her to offset any harm that could come to her or the baby. Alicia did not. When her baby boy was born, it had an inexplicable deformity. The infant had a large tumor on his neck. Doctors did not know how to treat it. The aunt said, "Que te dije? What did I tell you? I knew this could happen. You looked up at the moon!"

It is claimed that when there is a full moon, accidents increase and hospital visits rise. Some say aberrant behavior also takes place. The word *lunatic*, a wildly foolish person, comes from the Latin word *luna*, which is also Spanish for "moon." The moon was worshipped as a deity in some ancient cultures. The moon intrigued the Indians of New Mexico. A few researchers believe some tribes synchronized and aligned their structures with the moon and the universe. The moon was associated with magic. A moonbow is like a rainbow. One can appear at night, opposite in the sky where the moon is visible. People thought the moon could bring up terror, fright and madness and could signal foreboding events that could happen.

5

CHILDREN OF THE STARS

Creation myths and legends from ancient civilizations around the world can be both curious and puzzling. Experts try to fit what is known in the world as far as history and the development of cultures into a convenient and chronological time frame. When something arises that challenges preconceived notions and when reasoning and ingenuity simply cannot solve multiple questions, then artifacts and existing evidence are cast aside. However, it is the mystery that surrounds objects, ruins, structures, sightings and accounts that captures the imagination.

Some ancient civilizations test the boundaries of science, especially when it comes to beliefs in their origins. For example, the Hopi Indians of New Mexico and Arizona firmly hold that their direct ancestors came from the Pleiades, the place in the stars. They call their ancestors the Chuhukon, "those who cling together." This is taken as a reference to the star cluster in the heavens. The Pleiades are depicted on a kiva wall in Chaco Canyon. The Dagon people in Africa claim their ancestors arrived on this earth from the Sirius star system. These dwellers of the sky came from the stars as spirits they say. Sirius A can be seen with the naked eye, but Sirius B and its orbital period were described by the Dagon to anthropologists before the star's discovery. This did not occur until the 1950s, with the use of an advanced telescope. This revelation has been strongly contradicted by experts, however; Sirius B is represented in four-hundred-year-old artifacts of the Dagon.

A prevalent ancient myth that is held in New Mexico and elsewhere in the world is that a race of superhumans existed at one time. This is not given

New Mexico Indian dancers perform a spiritual dance circa 1949. At times, Native Americans portrayed gods, underworld spirits, wildlife and other life forms in dances.

much credibility. It is said that these humans built much of what modern men cannot understand or comprehend. Ancient super civilizations in legend include the famous lost culture of Atlantis. It is still being searched for, to no avail. During the thirteenth century, Venetian merchant and traveler Marco Polo recorded fantastic stories. Engaging the silk trade with Asia, he journeyed to China, Japan and India. The famous explorer wrote about the belief of the third eye in India, elephants and a many-armed goddess and other strange god figures, including one with an elephant head. Polo wrote about unusual remedies and the strange things that people ate. The most fantastic for the times and even today involved mind over matter. At the court of the Kublai Khan, the Mongolian emperor, Marco Polo saw examples of levitation. Black magicians lifted objects up with mere thoughts. Astrologers could supposedly conjure up storms. Rocks were burned to provide heat. Polo was, of course, charged with heresy and taken before the Inquisition. He was imprisoned. Now we know he was describing coal.

New discoveries are continually being made that point to the progression of mankind further and further back even in New Mexico. The existence of cities and settlements that were covered by the waters of the oceans and by other natural elements such as volcanoes and ice continue to be discovered. Perplexing mysteries that have escaped logical explanations include the methods used to quarry, cut, shape and transport stones weighing up to many tons from ten miles up to one hundred miles to a particular site. How were these stones lifted and stacked to create the pyramids of Egypt, the monolith of Stonehenge and the statues of Easter Island? How about the puzzling structures at Machu Picchu built by the Incas? This was accomplished without the use of mortar, and the stones were cut and fitted so perfectly that a razor blade cannot be fit between the stones. Anthropomorphic beings are depicted on cliffs and stones in New Mexico and all over the world. The Nazca plains of Peru have depictions of animals and other things so large that they can only be seen from the sky while looking down. Huge stone spheres are found in Guatemala and neighboring areas. Some of these huge balls weigh tons. No one knows why these massive items were made and by whom. Some mysterious articles are found in the middle of nowhere.

A centuries-old New Mexico Indian pot shard with a circular-sphere of influence. Native American tradition claims this symbol relates to a genealogy with the cosmos.

On one of my many explorations south of Albuquerque, I came upon large river stones that had been placed in a spiral formation on the ground. Ancient Native Americans apparently placed these rocks. The stones were arranged around a fixed center with increasing distance from the center. Interestingly, this same design is found on petroglyphs, which are lines or carvings made by prehistoric people. This pattern is found in pottery produced by Indians in New Mexico centuries ago. This exact strange artistic form is found depicted by ancient cultures all over the world. Some researchers attribute a religious ritual significance to the portrayals of mystifying circles on stone and clay. Other things that baffle our understanding of human civilization can be found in New Mexico.

What is believed to have been a Native American ritual center can be found at Chaco Culture National Historical Park. Ancestral Pueblo Indians constructed a building at a site called Pueblo Bonito, "beautiful town" in Spanish, from about AD 828 to 1126. Chaco Canyon is located in western New Mexico. In this structure, which extends up to five stories high, there are thirty-two remains of kivas (large circular buildings with most of the structure underground). The actual use of kivas is still in dispute; however, it is generally believed they served a function during intense religious rites. The diameters differ, but some were up to forty feet or more. Access could be gained through the roofs by protruding ladders that led into the kivas and the rooms of the rest of the ancient horseshoe construction. Ventilator shafts conducted air into the lower parts of the chamber. The masonry walls formed benches about a foot wide and close to the floors inside. The dirt floors had holes going deeper into the earth. These were called *sipapus* and considered entrances into the spirit world. Native American lore related the spirits of their ancients emerged from the depths to populate the surface during their genesis. It was discovered that the Great Chaco Kiva Sanctuary at Chetro Ketl was constructed over a much earlier one. Deep archaeological digs found ten undisturbed sealed crypts in the walls. Strings of beads measuring ten to seventeen feet in length with 17,454 individual beads were exposed. This find was a major one.

Current scholarship suggests Pueblo Bonito was built in alignment with the North Star. It is now thought the builders were well aware of both solar and lunar cycles. These are marked in petroglyphs on adjacent cliff walls. For about three hundred years, Pueblo people used twelve major structures that appear to be perfectly aligned with the sunrise, sunset, moonrise and the phases of the moon. Complex astronomical alignments and celestial patterns in the construction of these prehistoric ruins confound experts. In this center of astronomy and cosmology there was knowledge of an order in the universe. This highly sophisticated culture produced other mysteries.

A circular Pueblo Indian kiva entrance into the underground spirit world. The hidden anthropological mystery of kivas remains unexplained.

A centuries-old Indian basket carrier and a seagull on pottery shards found in New Mexico.

There was an extensive system of roads that connected a spreading network of Indian settlements. In a landscape of around thirty thousand square miles, some estimated forty thousand people lived, worked and prayed. Here native engineers built a four-hundred-mile system of roads in a time when the wheel hadn't yet been invented. Some areas of the perplexing road are up to thirty feet wide. These roads are flanked by what are believed to be astronomical observatories. There are towers and stone complexes erected near the roads by these people. Archaeological digs at Pueblo Bonito thus far have made more mystifying discoveries. Cylindrical clay jars demonstrate there was direct contact with the Indians of Central America, where these jars were manufactured. Remnants of cacao, which comes from a tropical evergreen tree, have been found at Pueblo Bonito. The tree bears reddish-brown seedpods. Aztec Indians used these pods to produce a thick cocoa that was drunk during religious ceremonies. Parrot feathers have also been found. This proves that the Indians located in this area of New Mexico had contact with other advanced civilizations in the Americas—perhaps even the Mayans, who built observatories to study the stars.

Interestingly, Native Americans claim the ancients were in direct contact with extraterrestrials. According to legend, these alien beings came from

Unusual artifacts and unexplained objects have been found in archaeological sites where they shouldn't be.

above as spheres of light. They say these luminescent spheres continue to visit and interact with humans. Indians in the past produced sacred songs devoted to protecting them from these round objects or balls of light. Native Americans have called these balls of light spirit orbs or spirit guides meant to direct us.

There is a certain mysterious and puzzling kind of stone that was used by shamans who purportedly mediated between this world and the spirit world. These rocks have been called shaman stones, vortex stones, thunder balls, Hopi marbles and Moqui balls. Some scientists refer to them as "cosmic spherules." In 2004, American Mars rovers called *The Spirit* and *Opportunity* sent back images of similar stones. These unusual rocks have been called "blueberries." They are round and appear in groups. Those found on earth have an outer shell of hematite and a sandstone or hollow center.

Ancient mystery stones prized by Indians. A vessel, bone, shards and Moqui stones add to the strange. At lower left, two dark orbs resemble those found on Mars.

A vortex stone. These rare and eerie stones were created by liquid rock whirling around an axis. Experts are at odds explaining perplexing and persistent mysteries.

Hematite is a reddish mineral that is the main ore of iron. Scientists say the cosmic spherules were formed by the ablation of meteorites. Ablation is the dissipation of heat generated by atmospheric friction. Other scientists propose a more mundane theoretical explanation: the natural shifting of water and sand through the ages caused these ordinary stones to form. However, scientists are in a quandary to answer how similar stones formed on Mars, unless there was sand and water on the planet. They are still searching for answers.

Native Americans in New Mexico have an ancient answer. According to the legends and lore of the Hopi Indians, the strange stones are a visible connection between the cosmos, the spirit world and the natural world. The Hopi were called the Moqui by the early Spanish explorers. These Indians were found in the modern states of New Mexico, Arizona, Colorado, Nevada, California, Texas and Utah, parts of which composed New Mexico territory under the Spanish government. The Hopi tribe is considered to be the progenitor of all of the Pueblo Indians. In the Hopi language, *Moqui* means "those that left us for the world beyond." Hopi legend claims that the spirits of their dead ancestors return and play marbles with the living by using these thunder balls during the night. At daybreak, this interaction between the living and the dead ends, and the spirits return back to the heavens.

Moqui stones have many unusual forms. Some are grooved spheres with ridges around the circumference. Others are cylindrical hollow pipes. Most are round or elliptical in shape. Some describe the oval shapes as resembling unidentified flying objects. The puzzling rocks have also been called star stones. They have been said to protect one from Evil Eye. They have also been used in rituals to supposedly contact extraterrestrials. It is claimed that humans can use these sacred stones for astral journeying. These stones range in age from 25 million years to 190 million years, during the beginning of the Jurassic period. Indian medicine men in New

A Moqui Star Stone. These unusual rock formations have contiguous encircling shapes. Hopi Indians prozed these stones as connections to extraterrestrials.

Mexico used Moqui stones for meditation and healing. It is thought there are male elliptical stones that hold positive energy and female round stones holding negative energy. One must hold a gendered pair in each hand. Sometimes these stones will change color. They can help in overcoming the fear of death. Sacred Indian stones can also help in spiritual enlightenment and physical and mental healing. The Hopi Indians also produced Kachina images, pine and cottonwood polychromed statues representing spirits of their deities. Ancient Native American mystics in New Mexico believed in a direct communion with the sun, moon, stars and the universe. The Children of the Stars still hold many secrets waiting to be discovered.

II

MYSTICAL MISSIONS

6

SPIRIT MASTERS

Por aquí paso la Muerte   *Death passed by here*
Con un manojo de velas,   *With a bunch of candles,*
Preguntando a los enfermos   *Asking the sick,*
¿Como les va de viruelas?   *How is it going with the smallpox?*

Some people in New Mexico have been asked, "Can you tell me something about the Santa Muerte cult?" Ignorance promotes ignorance. When this absurd question is asked, this means the one asking knows little or nothing at all about New Mexico's Hispanic culture. To clarify, hopefully once and for all, Santa Muerte is an anomaly from Mexico. This highly irregular idiosyncratic belief has to do with the abnormal worship of death by those involved with the drug trade in Mexico and other Latin American countries. This has absolutely nothing to do with New Mexico. The idea of Santa Muerte may be a strange but logical offshoot of the annual Día de los Muertos celebration in Mexico. However, this homage to death as a saintly figure with its own chapels, altars, decorated figures and prayers is primarily unique to Mexico.

New Mexico pretty much followed the idea of death as transplanted and introduced into the territory by early Spanish colonists as it existed during the European Middle Ages during widespread epidemics. Death is the master of our certain demise; therefore, faith should prevail and prepare one for a joyous afterlife. In New Mexico, death was personified as La Doña Sebastiana. The Angel of Death is depicted replete with a scythe, bow and

Above: *La Muerte Llama (Death Calls)*. *Print from* La Doctrina Cristiana, *La Revista Católica Publishing Company, Las Vegas, New Mexico, 1889.*

Opposite: *La Bruja (The Witch)*, by Ray John de Aragón. Belief in witches has been widespread in New Mexico since the Spanish colonial period.

arrows or hatchet and always riding in a "death cart." Death is a spirit master that controls our mortality. The idea of a death cart may have had its origins from the large horse carts used during medieval times. During that period of absolute pandemic misery in Europe, bodies were placed outside houses each morning and picked up by men who piled them up in wagons to be buried in mass graves. These were heart-wrenching times.

From about the tenth to the eighteenth centuries, Europeans believed in witchcraft, various demons and supernatural beings. Engravings, woodcuts and paintings depicted interpretations of apocalyptic horsemen, evil spirits, religious-political devilry, witchcraft and sorcery. Hans Holbein, who created a *Dance of Death* alphabet, and Albrecht Durer's *Knight, Death and Devil* illustrate the preoccupation with life and death. Memento mori, tokens of

Macabre Dance of the Dead, Cologne, 1489. A medieval theme personified death as the universal skeleton.

those who died, were prized. Reckoning and resurrection were also shown in dance, music and parades. The ballad "Acuérdate, Mortal" (Remember Mortal) shows how this belief system was carried into New Mexico and other Spanish colonies:

Acuérdate, mortal,	*Remember, mortal,*
el fin fatal	*the fatal end*
del sepulcro el horror	*the tomb and the horror*
do te encaminas;	*toward which you are traveling;*
contempla con temor;	*contemplate and tremble;*
así solo sabrás	*that way you will know how to*
aprovechar la vida.	*profit from life.*
Hombres, debéis morir,	*Men, you will die,*
debéis morir,	*you will die;*
pensad en bien vivir.	*think of being good.*
Riqueza, dignidad,	*Riches, dignity,*
es vanidad	*it's all vanity*
tu falaz pompa:	*your fraudulent pomp:*
todo viene a parar,	*all will come to an end,*
¡Cuan amargo pesar!	*Oh what bitter grief!*
En la estrecha mansión del	*In the brief journey of*
féretro sombrío.	*the darkened hearse.*

Gracia y saber,	*Grace and knowledge,*
inexorable,	*relentless,*
en gusano y fetor,	*in worm and stench,*
encenizas y horro	*in ashes and horror,*
cambias, muerte cruel, sin	*you will change, cruel death,*
que a nadie perdones.	*without forgiving anyone.*

Various feminine names were used for artistic wooden renderings of death in New Mexico: La Doña Sebastiana, the Venerable Lady; La Comadre Sebastiana, the Venerable Godmother; and La Huesuda, the Bone Lady. Death images in New Mexico were carved wooden skeletons with protruding ribs and gray or white horsehair. Sometimes actual human hair was used. Obsidian or mica was used for the eyes, or they were simply hollowed-out. The images were either toothless or had human teeth. The death figures were often dressed in black and wore black shawls. The carts resembled the full-sized wooden supply carts brought into the New World by the Spanish explorers and settlers. At times, large wooden carts meant for use during Lenten Vía Crucis processions were pulled by Penitentes. These two-wheeled vehicles are considered an art form unique to New Mexico. The oldest extant *carreta* (cart) dates to the Civil War era; however, earlier ones may have simply crumbled or parts were used for others once they were worn and useless.

It was obvious that people believed the Grim Reaper most often appeared during nighttime. Ill fate, or death, took place frequently at midnight or late at night. One could be captivated or placed under the power of witches or others by the use of magic, spells or other unnatural means. For some reason, there was a fascination with the hour of twelve dating back centuries in Western cultures. The Spanish in New Mexico called this *la mala hora* (the bad hour). They transformed this short phrase into *la malora* or *la malogra* for the name of a witch or wicked spirit that could wait for you at crossroads and take you with it if you are out late at night in places you shouldn't be.

Native Americans in New Mexico believed in *mashishis*, soothsayers who could predict or foretell the future. Spanish descendants of early colonizers called women with this ability *adivinadoras*. There was a certain fear of fortunetellers. Indians felt medicine men and shamans had certain supernatural powers to cure the body, heart and soul.

Early Spanish New Mexico folk stories revolve around unexpected appearances of the Angel of Death. She can be around when we least expect

A Zuni Pueblo medicine man blows sacred smoke into symbols of culture and traditions serving as passages into beliefs. *From Samuel W. Cozzens,* The Marvelous Country, *Boston, 1876.*

it. Some of the tales are scary; others, like the story of Miguel and Cleotilda, were meant to teach a simple lesson.

Miguel and his wife, Cleotilda, were quite excited. She had given birth to a healthy boy. Senobia, the well-known partera from Ojitos Fríos twenty-five miles away, had delivered the infant. She then returned home. After a few days, the young couple knew they had to see the nearest priest to have the baby baptized. But there was a problem. They lived out in the middle of nowhere. The nearest neighbors lived many miles away, and they had no idea who to ask to serve as godparents. Miguel got an idea. "I'll ride out on the road and ask the first person I see and beg the one I meet up with to serve as a godparent for Joselito." They had chosen the name of José, which was the name of the mother's great-grandfather.

It didn't take long for Miguel to find an old woman who was walking along with a cane. He didn't know it was Death in the flesh. They say Doña Sebastiana can change her appearance in an instant. Anyway,

Carreta de La Muerte (*Death Cart*) by Ray John de Aragón. To illustrate their mortality, Spanish settlers in New Mexico created death images.

Death was not only surprised with the request but also overjoyed, since no one had ever asked her for such an unusual favor. She served as the godmother and even fooled the village priest, who asked, "Where did you meet such a fine lady?" It didn't take long for Miguel to discover who this old woman was. But she was so kind and nice that she gave Miguel a magical power. He would be given the ability to save the lives of those at their deathbeds. She told the shocked father, "When I appear to claim someone, if I'm at the foot of the bed, you can save the person. However, if I'm standing by the headboard, I'm taking the person." The arrangement worked out perfectly, but then Miguel was at the home of a dear friend who did not want to die yet. Miguel found himself in a quandary. What could he do?

Godmother Sebastiana appeared and stood by the head of the bed. Miguel had moved his friend around so that his head was at the foot of the bed, and the feet were at the head of the bed. The Death Angel got confused, and Miguel quickly saved his friend. Needless to say, she was not very happy. But what goes around comes around. The Death Angel took Miguel into another room and showed him two lit candles. She told the perplexed young man, "See this tall candle and this short one? One has a high strong flame, and the other has a short weak one. The tall one was for you, and the short one was for your friend. Now things have been switched. He will live, and you will die. I'll go to your home for you tomorrow at twelve midnight. Be ready. Say your prayers."

Miguel went home, trembling. He told his wife about what had happened. She had no idea what he could do to save himself, but he was quite smart. Miguel came up with a plan that was foolproof. He had a long beard and long curly hair. He shaved his face and cut his hair. Since he had bushy eyebrows he trimmed those too. But that wasn't all; he had his wife dye his hair. Since he was thin and lanky, he tied a pillow around his waist and put on some big clothing that had belonged to his father. He told his wife to tell the Death Angel that he had gone into town and would be returning soon and to say that her cousin Felipe was visiting. "So you're Felipe?" Death asked. "Yes, I am," Miguel answered. "So what are you doing here?" "I'm just visiting my cousin Cleotilda." Miguel was quite content, eating a bowl of beans and chile. He would take pieces of tortilla, shape these into spoons, pick up his food and stuff it into his mouth. "That looks muy delicioso," Death said. "Yes, it certainly is; in fact, I'm getting another bowl. Do you want some?" "No, thank you," the feared angel answered. "I don't eat much."

Anyway, the Grim Reaper got tired of waiting. She conceded, "It's getting quite late, and Miguel hasn't returned. I have to figure something out quick. I think I'll just take Felipe. He had a good meal, and I think Miguel wouldn't mind." As you can imagine, Miguel's eyes opened wide as a piece of meat stuck in his throat and he choked to death. It was the stroke of midnight.

7

A HOLY GHOST

Nuevo Mexico is an enchanted land that holds many unusual mysteries. One that is most perplexing and intriguing is actually recorded in the annals of its ancient history. This strange mystery comes out of the seventeenth century, and it affected a powerful king for the rest of his life. It had already touched thousands of native people in the vast territory of New Mexico. This mind-boggling happening still continues to stun both researchers and scholars. Dyed-in-the-wool skeptics attempt to come up with ideas to cast off what took place. It is still unexplained.

The following profound words maintain certain beliefs and perceptions that people in New Mexico believed to be true: "Santo que no hace ruido es mas grande su poder." (A saint who makes no sounds has greater powers.)

Sor María de Agreda stood firm as she faced endless questions from officials of the Spanish Inquisition who read what she had written:

> *I should not be astonished to hear myself condemned as audacious, foolhardy and presumptuous by any person who will begin to realize (if realized it can be) that I, a simple woman, who is of herself but sheer weakness and ignorance…has resolved and attempted to write of divine and supernatural things.*

In his *Memorial*, an account of what he had experienced in New Mexico, in 1630, Fray Alonso de Benavides wrote:

We immediately dispatched the said Fray Salas, with another companion, who is the Fray Diego Lopez; whom the…Indians went with as guides. And before they went, we asked the Indians to tell us the reason why they were with so much concern petitioning us for baptism, and for Religious to go to indoctrinate them. They replied that a woman like that one whom we had there painted—which was a picture of the Mother Luisa de Carrión [the superior of a religious order of nuns]—*used to preach to each one of them in their own tongue, telling them that they should come to summon the Frays to instruct and baptize them…and that the woman who preached to them was dressed precisely like her who was painted there; but that the face was not like that one, but that their visitor was young and beautiful.*

Fray Benavides wrote about the frays who were going out to minister to the Indians and what occurred when the leader walked up to them:

And on the third day they ran upon the Religious, whom they asked to show them the picture of the woman that used to preach to them. And when the Fray showed him the picture of Mother Luisa de Carrión, they said she was dressed like that one…and immediately went to give the news

White Sands, New Mexico. Mysterious footprints have appeared on the gypsum granules for centuries. Following them has led to getting lost. *Photo by Ramón Juan Carlos de Aragón.*

to their people....And they came out to meet them in procession with two crosses in front as they were so well instructed....The frays took their two Crucifixes...and all came to venerate it...and the same they did to a very pretty infant Jesus that the frays carried, putting their mouth and eyes to his feet with much devotion...then more than ten thousand souls having come together in that field to hear the word of the Lord, the Fray Salas...A marvelous thing!...For with one great cry all uplifted their arms, rising to their feet, asking for the holy Baptism...and that which most hath moved us to compassion is that the mothers who had in their arms their tiny children at the breast, seeing them incapable of performing this action, took them by their little arms and held them upward....For, it being three o'clock in the afternoon when they commenced, they had to bring sick ones all afternoon, all night, and the next day until ten o'clock...with only making the sign of the Cross and saying the Gospel of St. Luke...the prayer of Our Lady... and that of Our Father St. Francis...instantly they rose up well of all their infirmities, the blind, lame, dropsied, and of all their pains....The soldiers who saw it were as stunned to see so many marvels.

Sometime in 1626, Fray Alonso de Benavidez, a Catholic Franciscan priest, was appointed *custos* (custodian) of the mission churches and first agent of the Inquisition in New Mexico. He was born on the island of San Miguel in the Azores. In 1602, he entered the Order of Friars Minor in Mexico City, the capital of New Spain. In the far northern frontier of Nueva España, Benavidez sought to establish new missions and convert the Indian tribes. The colony had been established in 1598, around thirty-two years earlier. The famous fray labored in New Mexico for around three years. Fray Alonso is credited with taking the famous and oldest Marian wooden religious statue with him to Santa Fe. This image is popularly known as La Conquistadora, or Nuestra Señora de la Santa Fe (Our Lady of the Holy Faith). There is a religious confraternity in Santa Fe that honors this designation of Mary, the mother of Christ, as the Protector of New Mexico.

King Philip II of Spain set up the duties of the inquisitor in 1569 when he organized a tribunal of the Inquisition in Mexico City. Inquisitors were to seek out heretics and those who broke the canon laws of the Catholic Church. This was a judicial system with judge/inquisitors who questioned and then convicted offenders, who would then be punished. Many who were tried were found innocent, but some were found guilty. The guilty sometimes included governors who were stripped of their authority and were cast out of the kingdom to isolated areas. For example, Spanish governors in the New

View of Pecos Ghosts. Ruins provide us with a portal to see things as they once were and are, such as at Pecos National Monument. *Photo by Lucia Dolores de Aragón.*

World were bound to protect and respect the rights of the Indians as Spanish citizens. Fray de Benavidez could impose various punishments, such as pilgrimages to holy sites. Offenders might have to carry a cross for all to see. Black magic, ghosts and witches had to be deflected somehow. Malevolent practices were punished by confession, repentance and charitable work, such as caring for the sick, elderly and infirm. Between 1626, and 1629, Fray de Benavidez's scribe took his pen and dipped it in black ink.

He recorded something fantastic.

It seems that a group of Indians called the Jumanos from an area known as Las Salinas—the lands of salt on the eastern plains of New Mexico—told an astonishing story. The extraordinary tale goes that a group of Spanish priests traveled on a mission and that many natives came up to welcome them. The leader and others walked up, bowing and ecstatic. They knelt and kissed the priests' robes and their crosses. They not only knew the Franciscans were coming but also when they would appear. The friars were stunned when the Indians told them that a beautiful woman dressed in blue appeared among them. She spoke their language although she was not one of their tribe. She also knew about their customs and rituals. Her calming voice assured the Indians there was nothing for them to be afraid of. Some of the warriors wanted to kill her, but when she was threatened with the loss of her life, she held out her hand with an extremely friendly and peaceful gesture. The braves froze in their tracks, so she was allowed to walk among them.

The woman in blue said she was sent to save their souls and convert them to the Christian faith. She would go on to appear many times, not only to this tribe but to others as well. When she left, she would walk over a ridge. Some of the Indians followed her, but she mysteriously disappeared. The strange woman loved the children. She also had a gift for healing. News about her traveled rapidly from one area to another. At first, Fray Alonzo de Benavides simply dismissed the whole thing as fanciful tales. Besides, he was much too busy establishing new mission churches to give the stories any credibility. The inquisitor's administrative duties kept him preoccupied with the spiritual needs of the Indians. However, the persistent rumors and reports of a miracle that was taking place kept him awake at night.

While back in Spain to provide a report to the king about religious successes in New Mexico, Fray Benavidez received interesting news. Someone informed him that he should seek out the mother superior at the convent at Agreda. He immediately set out for the convent after he completed his business at the royal court. He succeeded in meeting with Sor María de Agreda, the abbess vwho served as the superior of the nuns. Under questioning, the sister finally admitted to the stunned fray that she had the ability to bilocate to New Mexico territory. She never left Spain. He did not believe her at first, but then she began to provide him with detailed descriptions of the places she visited and the natives she saw and met with. She described the Jumanos, or the Salineros, Indians who mined salt deposits in Las Salinas. They were salt traders who were often attacked by Comanche, Apache and Navajo raiders. Sor María talked about their appearance, what they wore and spoke to all of the Indians she met in their own languages.

In her translation of Fray Benavidez's *Memorial*, Mrs. Edward E. Ayer notes:

On the last of April 1631, Benavides visited the now-celebrated Mother María de Jesús, abbess of the Convento de la Concepción Purísima in the town of Agreda, on the borders of Aragon and Castile. This visit, which seems to have covered a fortnight, was made at the instance of Father-General Siena, who had informed Benavides, those eight years before he had notice of this remarkable woman, of how she had apparitions and

La V. M. Maria de Jesus de Agreda. Predicando a los Chichimecos del Nuebo-mexico.

Left: Sor María de Jesús de Agreda, Fray Alonso de Benavidez, revised *Memorial 1630*. Mother Superior María de Agreda mysteriously bilocated to New Mexico from Spain.

Below: Mission Church at Abo. Many have claimed strange experiences at the church ruins and area. *Photo by Lucia Dolores de Aragón*.

Venerable María de Jesús de Agreda miraculously appeared and preached to the Indians. Engraving by Antonio de Castro, in Tanto Que se Saco, Benavides, Mexico, 1730.

revelations concerning the conversions in New Mexico, and had himself made the nun a personal visit. Benavides, who mentions Mother María de Jesús somewhat at length in the Memorial in connection with his description of the conversion of the Jumano Indians, now learned that this ascetic, who was about twenty-nine years of age, had made numerous "flights" to New Mexico, commencing eleven years before, sometimes making the journey three or four times in twenty-four hours. The miracles she claimed to have performed were marvelous in the extreme. Benavides received from her a hand writing, dated May, 15, 1631, attesting to the truth of her assertions; he also obtained "the very habit which she wore when she made those visits, and the veil about which there is a peculiar odor that comforts the soul."

María de Jesús de Agreda was born on April 2, 1602, in the village of Agreda, near Tarazona, Spain. She was the daughter of Francisco Coronel and Catalina de Arana. She entered the convent of the Inmaculada Concepción of the discalced Franciscan nuns in 1617 at the age of fifteen. She took her vows in 1618. In 1625, she was selected as the abbess of

Exploring the ruins of Quarai mission church around 1930. This and other sites where María de Agreda appeared through bilocation were places where churches were built.

the convent. The nun's professed appearances through bilocation in New Mexico began around 1623, when she was twenty-one. Her fame as a capable religious leader spread far and wide, and both secular and church leaders for advice soon consulted her. Sor María de Agreda became the confessor of King Philip IV.

What appeared to be outrageous stories and claims became steadily more fantastic. Fray Benavidez was a high-ranking inquisitor of the church. What could he do? The nun was intensely questioned; especially since she worked on a series of writings she called *The Mystical City of God*. Interestingly, no documents or records seem to exist that point to what followed her miraculous appearances in New Mexico. The mystery remains. Sor María also claimed she had been around when frays visited with and ministered among the Indians and could repeat some of the words that were said by them. Sor María de Jesús de Agreda died on May 24, 1665. Pope Clement X declared the nun venerable in 1673. Her life and career led to her being declared New Mexico's saint, the "Great Marian Mystic." However, none of the popes who followed Pope Clement have canonized her. She is called the Blue Nun in New Mexico and still has a large and dedicated following in the state.

8

A Mystical Hermit

Though I walk through the Valley of Darkness, I fear no evil.
—Psalm 23:4

Elba C. de Baca, a folklorist from Las Vegas, New Mexico, had an important copy of *El Independiente* (*The Independent*) newspaper, of Las Vegas, New Mexico, dated 1898. In her *Legends of a Hermit*, an undated booklet without copyright, she mentions this following story from that issue, handed down to her from her father:

> *East of El Porvenir is an enormous, majestic peak named by the people "El Cerro del Ermitaño" (Hermit's Peak). A very holy hermit lived in a cave there from the year 1863 until the year 1867. His name was Giovanni Maria Agostiniani. All may see the cave where he lived....The hermit devoted his life to prayer and penance. Everyone who knew him admired him greatly. He was devoted to our Blessed Mother and to the Passion of Our Lord. This place became a pilgrimage for the faithful. This holy man organized a society or confraternity whose main obligation was to go up to the peak on the second of May—the eve of the Holy Cross—and on the first Sunday of September. On these dates, they were to pray the rosary, the Stations of the Cross, and other prayers. Before he left, he asked the members to remain faithful to God and to continue with their devotions. To this day descendants of the original members have remained faithful to their promise. The hermit was quoted as saying, "I must leave because I*

Roman Catholic faith provided spiritual needs of the Spanish settlers in New Mexico. The cross and God served them. *Photo by Ramón Juan Carlos de Aragón.*

Hermit Giovanni Maria Agostiniani, nineteenth-century engraving. The hermit became a popular resident of northern New Mexico, recognized as a healer and prophet.

have made a vow never to remain too long in one place. I am not a prophet, neither am I the son of a prophet, but one thing I assure; in the future this place will be a site of many signs and wonders. My days are numbered. Please pray for me."

In September 1965, I enrolled for classes at New Mexico Highlands University in Las Vegas. A major part of our freshman orientation was to climb Hermit's Peak and visit the old hermit's cave. It was an annual ritual for all incoming freshmen at the school. After bounding over large stones while following a winding trail for endless miles, we all reached the massive cave at the top of the peak. After hearing so much of the folklore told in northern New Mexico about this purportedly wondrous man, I was anxious to see the place. I stood awestruck. There was a fantastic view of New Mexico in all directions, and the open cave hid many amazing secrets. There were wooden crosses, reliquaries and prized mementos and an ancient fire pit. Followers of the hermit and visitors alike had left various unusual objects. This helped to set the scene for the following story.

Some time before the Civil War, legend relates that a man joined a wagon train at Independence, Missouri, bound for Santa Fe. It was a long and

Rare photo of Hermit Giovanni Agostiniani, circa 1865. The Brotherhood of the Hermit began in Las Vegas, New Mexico, after the departure and death of the hermit.

arduous trip along the Santa Fe Trail for all travelers, but it was especially so for this very strange person. Those who were concerned with his safety offered this striking man a ride in their wagons and on their horses. He had long hair and a beard and was dressed in a hooded flowing gray-black robe. The extraordinary man carried a long wooden staff. Bells were attached to it with weathered rawhide. When he walked alone, this solitary man's bells echoed through the valleys. His feet were bruised and covered with aged, toughened skin. He always refused the rides, saying he had to walk because he had a hard debt to pay. His barefoot travels with heavily worn sandals had already taken him through Spain, France and some Latin American countries. Now he headed toward New Mexico territory.

This eccentric and most unusual person was apparently born in Novara, Italy, around 1801. According to the lore of the period, Giovanni was the son of a wealthy Lombardy nobleman. He was well educated and learned several languages. At this point, history, legend and myth intertwine. After Giovanni killed a man in a duel, he decided to live a life of solitude and penance. He became a hermit and spent much of his time meditating and praying. Rather than travel all the way to Santa Fe, the hermit chose to remain near the town of Las Vegas. He found a secluded cave near Romeroville where he made his home. This was only temporary. Curious people sought him out, so he left, seeking another place. He heard about El Cerro del Tecolote, or the Owl's Peak, situated fourteen miles west of Las Vegas. It is a granite peak rising up to 10,500 feet. From time immemorial, this high peak served as a site of religious functions. Some *cerros* (hills) in New Mexico were used by the Penitente brotherhood as integral during Passion plays reenacting the suffering and death of Jesus Christ. To the Penitentes, these places rising above the land are used to reenact the Way of the Cross. The hills are symbolic of Mount Calvary on which the crucifixion and death of Jesus Christ took place. During Lent, El Cerro de Tome, near Albuquerque, is a popular site. Giovanni followed a long, winding trail to the top of the peak.

According to Guadalupe Gallegos y Baca and Juanita C. De Baca, during an interview with Elba C. de Baca, Don Miguel Romero played a substantial role during Giovanni's stay in the area. Don Miguel was a wealthy Las Vegas merchant and member of the powerful Romero family. His brother Benigno Romero is credited with providing the land, seed money and selfless energy for the creation of the New Mexico State Hospital. Dr. Lynn Perrigo wrote, "The need to which Don Benigno devoted his attention was for the improvement in the care of insane persons, who in those days customarily were locked up in jail and kept there interminably." Benigno and his wife were so concerned about those cast off by society that they sympathetically took men, women and children into their home. According to folklorists, it was Don Manuel Romero, captain of a wagon train full of merchandise from a trip to Council Grove, Kansas, who offered Giovanni safe passage to New Mexico. The nomad had apparently spent a short time in St. Louis, Missouri, and people saw him there as a religious missionary. Officials saw no problem with him going to New Mexico and provided the roaming vagabond with a paper of introduction signed by several prominent citizens.

Don Miguel Romero established a mercantile on the plaza in Las Vegas, New Mexico, in 1878. This business became one of the largest trading companies on the Santa Fe Trail. The well-known merchant maintained a continual flow of commercial wagons traveling to and from Missouri. The Romero family became successful to the point that his brother Hilario opened a bookstore with a significant stock of Spanish-language books near the Romero Mercantile. Benigno Romero organized a drugstore and sundry he called La Sanadora (the healer, or the healing place). As an early enterprising pharmacist, Benigno purchased and sold a variety of healing plants and roots for the treatment of illnesses and maladies. He sought out medicinal plants from Native Americans and published the first known book in New Mexico on the use and benefit of natural remedies. Benigno went so far as to package and bottle popular remedies and attempted to establish a market for these in the east. In the United States, medical practitioners were busy treating ailments with strange concoctions. Bear grease was used as an ointment. Deer dung and the excrement from other animals were ingredients in medicines. Opium and mercury were tried on patients. The ageless leeching of the sick, which was in widespread use in England, was still practiced by American physicians. This prompted the saying, "The cure is much worse than the illness." The enterprising Romeros were ahead of their time. Giovanni was exposed to this, but he also saw another side.

Don Margarito took the hermit into the family spread at Romeroville. This was an extensive area of pasturelands and livestock outside of Las Vegas. A huge house and sprawling ranch buildings complemented the setting. Giovanni was amazed with what he saw and began experiencing in New Mexico. The Romero family sought to protect Giovanni and support him after he related his life story and told them about his world travels. Margarito took the wandering hermit to El Cerro del Tecolote and showed him a large cave that the ecstatic hermit immediately made his home. There was a spring nearby to provide him with fresh water. Margarito was noted as the hermit's benefactor. The scrupulous merchant was well known for his charitable acts. Each year, he sponsored a massive Christmas party for needy children of all areas and gave the kids gifts. At one time, he hosted eight hundred children. Margarito introduced Giovanni to the Penitente Brotherhood, and the hermit became an active member, since his life was already filled with prayer and penance. Giovanni walked into town once a month for provisions. The walk would take days. He learned how to collect medicinal plants and roots plus piñon nuts and wild berries. He carried these in a burlap sack he strapped onto his back to sell in town. He would take beef jerky, dried fruit, beans, dried chilies and other goods back to the cave with him.

Others attempted to sell Margarito items for his mercantile business and especially for his La Sanadora pharmacy since information about his cures was rapidly spreading throughout the territory. A peddler from Missouri had a wagonload of products with literature that proclaimed:

> *"Parker's Tonic—The Best Health Restorer in the World."* *If you are miserable from dyspepsia, neuralgia, sour stomach, wakefulness, rising of the food, or yellow skin; if your blood is foul with humors* [a bodily fluid]

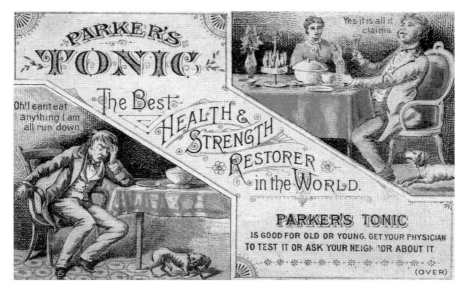

Snake oil peddlers introduced a variety of tonics meant to cure all illnesses with one bottle. Shady dealers infiltrated New Mexico.

and you have frequent pains in your head, back or limbs, your stomach, kidneys or liver is distressed, and there is no medicine on earth that will strengthen these debilitated organs as surely as Parker's Tonic. It will purify your blood, infuse energy into every part of the body, and is "A Perfect and Superlative Health Restorative."…In curing coughs, consumption, asthma, colds, and bronchitis, Parker's Tonic has met with astonishing success. It is a sure cure for indigestion, diarrhea, dysentery, rheumatism, chills, malaria, colic, and cramps, and has often saved life. It can never do any harm. One hundred dollars reward for a case it will not cure or help. Try it today, fifty cents and one dollar. Large saving buying one-dollar size.

Other imported products offered to Margarito and New Mexico merchants included Parker's Hair Balsam, which touted, "Never fails to restore the youthful color & beauty to gray and white hair." It is not officially known what went into the cure-alls that were sold by peddlers. Some suspect alcohol was in most, plus unpleasant items witches would have been accused of using in concoctions of the past. Some people actually became severely ill with the "elixirs of life," and a few even died. Many nefarious American con men tried to sell anything that would bring them a buck. When the hermit felt someone had bad intentions, such as these rogue merchants, it is said he always proclaimed, "You better start repenting right now, for I greatly fear you will be punished this very day!"

Giovanni became a legend in northern New Mexico. The hermit, however, left good memories with those he met. Giovanni Maria de Augustino (there are varying accounts of his surname) lived at the cave until 1867. Due to his wandering soul, he decided it was time for him to leave. Those he had touched with his kind words and respect, were filled with sorrow because he was so well liked and, in some circles, loved. Before the soulful hermit left, it was said he led all those who were gathered around him to an open grave. They were astonished when they saw it, especially when he said, "See this open grave? I have just this morning dug it. It symbolizes my own grave, for it will not be long ere I, too, will be lying in a similar grave. I want you to take turns coming up to El Cerro. I want you to check on this grave. When it is filled by unknown hands, know that my soul has already departed from this earth." With that, he left. It is written that Giovanni Maria then settled into a cave in the Organ Mountains in southern New Mexico, near Las Cruces. Around 1868, he was found dead in this dark, forbidding cave in the Organ Mountains. His body was filled with arrows and clutching

Calvario at Hermit's Peak, 1885. A group gathers during Lent at a Calvary with crosses commemorating the crucifixion of Christ. Some Calvarys were at highest points.

a crucifix. Legend claims that a band of Apaches found him on their sacred land. They saw him as a strange intruder who should not have been on their holy grounds. The story of the hermit does not end here. Things were happening back in Las Vegas.

It is claimed Don Margarito Romero started La Sociedad del Ermitaño, the Society of the Hermit. In May 1868, while celebrating La Exaltación de la Santisima Cruz (the Exaltation of the Most Holy Cross) with fellow Penitentes at the top of Owl's Peak, he had a vision of the filled-in grave of the hermit. Margarito became a leader of an annual pilgrimage to Hermit's Peak. On returning to town, he founded a society commemorating the life and deeds of the hermit. The Stations of the Cross up the mountain would be recited as always. They stopped at the top of the peak, where there were three crosses. Piñon wood luminarias were lit at the top to proclaim the ingrained faith of the people in Christ, as had been done for generations. But at the cave, they would discuss the hermit.

On September 3, 1908, the *Las Vegas Optic* reported:

> *Don Margarito Romero, head of the Brotherhood of the Hermit, led a party of priests and others to the summit of the towering mountain today and tonight the crest will be lighted by fires, beacons shining as tokens to the faithful. The night will be passed at the top of the crags and early morning mass will be chanted as the clouds roll away. Mr. Romero, as head of the Brotherhood of the Hermit, it is said to have received the mantle of the prophet, seer and saintly man who so long ago made his home on the top of the cliffs and proved to be a friend of all who inhabited this region.*

Benjamin Coca, a Montezuma, New Mexico resident who was a member of the Brotherhood of the Hermit since boyhood, recounted:

> *All of the members and their families went to visit the hermit's cave, as was the custom. At the cave, we lit wax candles, sang hymns and prayed. From the cave, we went from one cross to another. At each cross, measuring about six feet high by four and a half feet wide, we prayed two Lord's Prayers and two Ave Marías and prayers of the Holy Cross. There are fourteen crosses from the cave to the Calvary, a place where [there are] three maderos, huge pine beams that represent Christ's crucifixion. These crosses are located at the highest point of the peak and have been there since before New Mexico became a territory of the United States. To the south one can see Las Vegas and several other nearby towns. It is at this place that firewood luminarias*

The cave of Giovanni Maria Agostiniani, the Hermit, at Hermit's Peak near Las Vegas, New Mexico. The cave became a memorial site of annual pilgrimages.

are lit later at night. We returned to our camp from the Calvario to eat supper. After supper, we went back to the Calvary to pray. After praying the rosary and we received a blessing, we all returned to the camps. After talking about the hermit and drinking coffee for a while, we went up to the cave to light a luminaria. This is what the hermit did each night while he was there. This signified he was alive and well. Next, all of the brothers went to the freshwater spring after the luminaria burned out and the embers were extinguished. Tradition says the hermit found this spring by using witching for water. This was a method used in New Mexico since olden Spanish days.

Stream at foot of Hermit's Peak near Las Vegas, New Mexico. Legend claims the hermit touched the rocks and ground with his cane and created a stream of water.

Witching for water was the use of a divining rod. A forked hazel twig with two equal branches was cut, and the leaves were stripped off. The stump of the twig was cut to the length of five or six inches. Each branch was about fourteen inches. The ends of the branches were held with each hand. This was held in such a way that the stump of the twig projected straight forward. The elbows were bent and the forearms and hands extended. The knuckles were turned downward. The ends of the branches come out between the thumbs and base of the forefingers. The backs of the hands face up with the bottoms of the hands toward the body, a few inches apart. The mystic "witcher" walked over the ground exploring either for a vein of metal or source of underground water. The fork will spontaneously move if something is detected. The point of the stump rises and then falls, pointing down to what is being searched for. In New Mexico, divining was used since the colonial period, and many old-timers credited this method with discovering hidden springs. Benjamin Coca continued with his story:

> *We all went to the spring. Three women walked in front. We went along singing the alabado, hymn of Our Lady of Guadalupe. We finished the alabado when we arrived at the spring and we all knelt down. We removed*

our thick coats and shoes. I was bareback for my penitence. Water was poured over our heads, hands, arms and bodies. This water is ice cold even during the hottest days. After blessing ourselves, we mentioned the intention of each penance and the pouring of water. I said, "pour two pails of water over my head for the soul of my father, Carlos Coca." After our penance, which could last well over an hour depending on how many were there, we prayed the Stations of the Cross at each cross all the way back up to the crest. At the Calvario, we prayed the rosary and received a final blessing. This concluded the final devotion of the Brotherhood of the Hermit. We returned to the camps to saddle up our horses, load up our belongings and head home.

The majestic and imposing peak once known as El Cerro del Tecolote, Owl's Peak, was renamed Hermit's Peak. This commemorates Giovanni Maria's stay in northern New Mexico. The mystifying ritual dedicated to the hermit with the brotherhood continues.

9

ASCENDING SPIRITS

Once again, students asked a popular professor at the University of New Mexico, "Are you the real Indiana Jones?" The teacher, wearing the similar iconic hat and famous outfit portrayed in movies, simply smiled. In the highly acclaimed motion pictures, Harrison Ford, as a controversial archaeologist, leaves his classroom and students and goes off in search of fantastic lost civilizations. Among his peers, "Indie" is strongly opposed by "experts" in his work and efforts. They question his techniques and strenuously dispute his findings. Undaunted, Indiana Jones explores anyway. In real life, Dr. Frank C. Hibben mirrored the fictional character shown on film.

Frank Cumming Hibben was born in Lakewood, Cuyahoga County, Ohio, on December 5, 1910. His English ancestors settled in an area of Mount Pleasant, South Carolina. The family estate, called Hibben House, was built in 1755. The house still stands at number 111 Hibben Street on the Mount Pleasant side of the Charleston peninsula. Frank C. Hibben graduated from Princeton University in 1933. In 1940, he received a doctorate from Harvard University. During World War II, Hibben served as a commissioned officer and aide under Admiral Foy of the Joint Chiefs of Staff in Washington, D.C. He was on a plane shot down by a German submarine and was wounded. Dr. Hibben undertook secret missions for President Richard M. Nixon. He also worked with noted anthropologists Louis and Mary Leakey doing excavations in Kenya, Africa. The couple is credited with discovering some of the earliest evidence of human existence. Dr. Hibben became a professor of archaeology at the University of New Mexico.

Above: Setting up for an Indian or Spanish dig in New Mexico, circa 1922. Archaeologists and anthropologists searched for areas to explore.

Left: A prehistoric Indian ritual stone, with figure of a hunter and his bow and arrow. Spiritualists called for good hunting and success of warriors.

Sometime in 1936, Dr. Frank C. Hibben made a stunning discovery while exploring a cave in the Sandia Mountains. The cave is located on the steep sidewall of Las Huertas Canyon on the north side of the Sandias northeast of the city of Albuquerque. Here he found remains left by a primitive cave dweller. In an August 12, 1946 *Gallup Independent* article titled "New Mexico Cradled First Americans," reporter and writer J. Wesley Huff wrote:

> *The story of the Sandia Man was unfolded in four years of careful, diligent excavation during the years 1936 to 1940 by an expedition from the University of New Mexico under the direction of Dr. Frank C.*

A hand-held stone with a red iron oxide figure of a horse. When Spanish explorers entered New Mexico in 1540, Indians drew images of their horses.

Hibben. The results of this work were published in October 1941 by the Smithsonian Institution....Until the discoveries in Sandia Cave a few miles east of Albuquerque another New Mexico resident held the position as the first known American—Folsom Man.

He was named for the town of Folsom, NM, in the northeastern part of the state where first evidences of his culture were discovered....Chipping on down with sledgehammers and crowbars into the concrete—like mass under the travertine crust they found signs of human habitation. There were pieces of bone split to extract the marrow, and teeth of many animals. Scraps of flint and charcoal were scattered throughout the mass. There were scattered bones of the horse, extinct bison, and camel and teeth of the mammoth. Hunters had brought these bones into the cave to gnaw away the meat seared over their fires....[They] *encountered another layer in which were animal bones, flint, and the evidences of fire....*

After excavating deeper, Dr. Hibben was certain he had discovered evidence pushing the period of the earliest known man in America back by nearly twenty thousand years. However, controversy didn't fail to surround his claims, with some skeptics believing the famous archaeologist/anthropologist had salted his find with animal bones and artifacts. There was nothing to substantiate what they said, or claimed, but it was enough to cast some doubt on Hibben's work. What was even worse, his efforts were tainted by another spectacular story. The archaeologist claimed that in 1933, an old Indian led him to a curious artifact. The Indian said he made the discovery one day when he was traveling near sacred grounds on Isleta Pueblo land. This object is located 16.8 miles outside of the village of Los Lunas at the foot of "Hidden Mountain" in a remote area. Ancient writing in an extinct language appears on an eighty-ton slab of basalt about four and a half feet high. Harvard University scholar Robert Pfeiffer translated the writing. He said it appeared to be a copy of the Ten Commandments written in a Paleo-Hebrew script or in Cypriote Greek, which was used in the region of the Mediterranean Sea around 500 BC.

In the 1980s, during interviews I conducted with Dixie L. Perkins, an expert from Los Lunas, who wrote about the "Mystery Stone" or "Decalogue Stone," she supported Dr. Hibben but offered a different translation. She claimed the writing was the work of an ancient traveler named Zakyneros who was lost, and he chiseled in the writing to leave a record for those who would follow. This would be definitive proof predating pre-Columbian contact in the Americas by people from the Old World before Christopher Columbus.

Dr. Frank C. Hibben was notorious in his search for vanished cultures, mysterious artifacts and lost civilizations. Dr. Hibben became the director of the Maxwell Museum of Anthropology at the University of New Mexico. Hibben had his detractors and supporters. He was certain ancient

Fieldwork on an archaeological site in New Mexico, circa 1922. When artifacts found could not be logically explained, they were placed into forgotten boxes or lost.

explorers visited the New World long before Columbus, and these travelers, he ascertained, maintained a continuous contact with Native Americans in New Mexico and elsewhere. He set out to prove his theory and was ridiculed. Some said the archaeologist's dubious findings were nothing but hoaxes he perpetrated on a gullible public. They also asserted that no similar discoveries had been made in the United States. However, Dighton Rock, a forty-ton boulder in the Taunton River of Berkeley, Massachusetts, bore similar cryptic inscriptions and was discovered in 1690. A stone that has baffled investigators was found near the Platte River in Colorado. This rock also has what appears to be ancient Phoenician script. Unusual items have been found on the surface or in archaeological digs in America that shouldn't be there. Some experts have attempted to disprove these findings as hoaxes, but that has been very difficult to do, with supervised digs going down into the ground for up to ten or twenty feet in some cases. Perhaps, in time, Dr. Frank Cumming Hibben's dream about his astounding and extremely unconventional archaeological finds will be accepted and finally realized.

Sandia Cave was declared a National Historic Landmark in 1961.

10

PASSAGE TO STRANGENESS

Thy soul shall find itself alone
'Mid dark thoughts of the gray tombstone—
Not one, of all the crowd to pry
Into thine hour of secrecy.
—Edgar Allan Poe, "Spirits of the Dead"

Early Spanish settlers in New Mexico firmly believed that the dead could communicate with the living. The means of doing this is to hold the departed in one's memory. A highly unusual literary form in New Mexico recalled the deceased through *corridos del muerto* (ballads of the dead). These folk narrative poems, which were sung, recounted how the person died through their own words. Writers always had an introduction so those listening would know who died, the circumstances and their final goodbye.

Despedimiento de Raquel Ruiz	*The Goodbye of Raquel Ruiz*
Año de mil novecientos	*The year of nineteen*
Cuarenta y siete al entrar	*Forty-seven on entering*
El día cinco de enero,	*On the Fifth of January,*
No me quiero acordar.	*I don't want to remember.*
Raquel Ruiz viene conocida	*Raquel Ruiz comes well known*
Que en este lugar vivió	*From this place she lived*
En la esquina de una calle	*In a corner of a Street*
En San Miguel vivió.	*In San Miguel, where she lived.*

Hondo Canyon, New Mexico view. Arroyo Hondo was an ancient Spanish colonial area resplendent with stories about weird and eerie experiences.

This is the opening passage of a New Mexican ballad of farewell. The Spanish corrido is a poetic song accompanied by guitar that details the life of a person or a memorable event. The singer introduces the subject and then goes on to relate the story to the excited listeners. The history of corridos originates during the Spanish Middle Ages when roving minstrels or troubadours sang about romance and tragic heroic figures.

In Spanish colonial New Mexico, some local forms of these ballads developed. For example, when relating a story, folklorists introduced a traditional tale by saying, "Había una vez" (once upon a time). When singing a narrative song, the New Mexico singer sometimes used the word *cuando* (when) or *indita*. The word *indita* stems from *enditar*, meaning "indicates," or from which the story derives. "Esto indita lo que paso en ese día." (This indicates, or tells of, what happened on that day.) The actual word is *indicar* or *es indicativo*, but in New Mexico, singers simply said, "Esto indita," a transculturation of the pronunciation of *indica, lo que paso, o ocurrió* (what took place, or what happened). All of the early song telling in early Nuevo Mexico interrelate, are intertwined and are not disjointed, as are all of the Spanish traditions, heritage, culture, folklore and history.

Spine-chilling ballads from New Mexico remain to be studied. They appear to be unique to New Mexico. These ballads of despedimiento or farewell are buried in the sands of time. The bizarre, morbid, and frightening words comprise touching lyrics told from the perspective of the deceased, who sometimes does not want to say goodbye, but has no choice. What is hair-raising is that the recently departed is speaking to family and friends and is bidding an otherworldly farewell. Raquel Ruiz says she was murdered. It was an unsolved murder mystery. A very cold case! The reciter continues with his introduction so that the listeners will know the full story:

> *The inhuman Fermín Trujillo*
> *sees with the true God*
> *today, a holy commandment*
> *that says you shall not kill.*
>
> *God proclaimed his law*
> *so that it should be obeyed,*
> *under such stupidity.*
>
> *In the District Court*
> *your cause was decided*
> *and your life was saved.*

An ancient Spanish colonial cemetery with ruins of walls no longer extant. During the Spanish and Mexican periods, high walls were placed around graveyards.

Raquel Ruiz then goes on to recount how she spent the last moments of her life:

A la plaza fui apurada	*I went quickly to the plaza*
Ya se me pasaba el día	*For my day was passing,*
Ya la hora se me llegaba	*My hour was arriving*
Porque a si me convenía.	*Because that was committed.*
Mi hermanita iba conmigo	*My younger sister was with me*
Me vio cuando calli	*When she saw me fall*
Estaba en mi compañía	*She accompanied me*
Al momento que mori.	*The moment I died.*
Mis hijo y hermanos	*My children, my brothers,*
Mi mama llego apurada	*My mother arrived hurriedly,*
A la calle donde estaba	*To the street I was at,*
Alli me hallaron tirada.	*And they found me lying there.*
Lleno de nieve el camino	*The street full of snow*
El lugar donde calli	*The place I fell*
Sin esperanza de vida	*Without hope of life,*
Que a mi casa no volví.	*I never returned home.*

Adiós mis padres queridos	*Goodbye beloved parents*
No me volverán a ver	*You will see me no more*
Ya Dios no me dio licencia	*God has given me no license*
Para mi casa volver.	*To go back home.*
A mis cuatro hijos los siento	*I feel for my four children*
Mis padres con mas razón,	*My parents with just reason,*
Mis hermanos y parientes	*My brothers and relatives*
Sientan mi separación.	*All feel my separation.*
Adiós todos mis vecinos	*Goodbye my neighbors*
De todos me despido,	*To all I say farewell,*
sientan en sus corazones	*feel in your hearts*
y rueguen a Dios por mi.	*and pray to God for me.*
En los Estados Unidos	*In the United States*
Mi muerte publicaron,	*They published my death,*
En los radios y papeles	*On the radio and in papers*
A todo el mundo avisaron.	*They told the whole world.*
En mi vida respondía	*During my life I responded*
El nombre de Raquel Ruiz,	*With the name of Raquel Ruiz,*
Tuve una amiga querida	*I had a beloved friend*
Se llama Luz Ortiviz.	*Her name is Luz Ortiviz.*
Adiós todos mis amigos,	*Goodbye my friends,*
Adiós mis nietos queridos,	*Goodbye my beloved nephews,*
Adiós toda la gente,	*Goodbye all people,*
Yo de todos me despido.	*From all I beg my leave.*
Encomiendo a Dios mi alma,	*I commend my soul to God,*
De que se duela de mi,	*Who feels for me,*
Que a vistas del mundo entero,	*The whole world has seen,*
la muerte recibí.	*the death I received.*
En la calle fui tirada	*I was thrown into the Street*
Como la mas infeliz,	*As the most unfaithful,*
Pidan al eterno padre	*Ask the eternal father*
Por el alma de Raquel Ruiz.	*For the soul of Raquel Ruiz.*

The killer apparently went unpunished. One can gather that Raquel Ruiz was brutally murdered right in front of a younger sister. As a protagonist, she tells her own story. One can surmise that her best friend was somehow involved. Murder and intrigue abounds in this ballad. But this is only part of the spectral mystery.

Many who have had near-death experiences say they left their bodies and hovered over the area where they came close to death. They could see what was happening, who was there and hear what was said. If they revived and returned from the dead, they told their stories, but few have taken these people seriously. New Mexicans always maintained closeness with the deceased, so much so that they wrote many ballads from the perspective of the one who died, informing those who were to be left behind:

ADIÓS ACOMPAÑAMIENTO

*Adiós acompañamiento donde
    me estaban velando.
Ya se llego el tiempo de que me
    vayan sacando.
Adiós mis amados padres que
    conservaban mi vida.
Ya se llego el tiempo, ya se llego
    mi partida.
Que corazones no sienten tan
    solo en considerar que este
    paso tan amargo todos lo
    tienen que andar.
La sepultura es mi cama. La
    tierra mi propio ser.
Se me atemoriza el alma de
    considerarme en el.
Adiós todos mis amados
    parientes, toditos en general.
Encomienden mi alma a Dios,
    no me vayan olvidar.*

*Farewell my company where
    you were holding my wake.
My time has arrived for you to
    take me out.
Goodbye my beloved parents
    who preserved my life.
The time has arrived, the time
    for me to depart.
Which hearts do not consider
    that this bitter walk has to
    be done by all.
The grave is my bed. The dirt
    is my abode.
My soul is terrified in
    considering I will be in it.
Farewell beloved relatives, all
    of you.
Commend my soul to God, do
    not forget me.*

The dearly departed were never forgotten in New Mexico. Wakes for the dead were held in homes. Male and female lay religious penitentes prayed over the bodies encircled by lit candles, and they also recited special prayers

Entryway into Pecos Mission Church of Our Lady of the Angels built in the seventeenth century. Holy spirits have been seen. *Photo by Lucia de Aragón.*

Pilgrimage crosses at El Cerro. Crosses were placed on hills and mountains throughout New Mexico. *Photo by Lucia de Aragón.*

composed for the deceased while mentioning the person's names. Everyone dressed in black clothing. Women also wore black veils and, in early times, long black shawls. Those who passed away were not forgotten.

There is a curious death ritual preserved in New Mexico since the Spanish colonial period that still exists in some isolated areas today. It is the placing of an adobe mud brick or a rectangular small block of baked clay at the bare feet of the deceased in the coffin. A story is told that Saint Francis of Assisi was laid to rest with his feet up against a dried mud brick. Since the venerable saint had walked thousands of miles preaching and ministering during his life, this gesture was meant to place his mortal body into a holy communion with the earth. Saint Francis mortified his body with a disciplina, a leather whip. He experienced the wounds of the crucified Christ on his body.

Not surprisingly, when Spanish colonists established their capital in New Mexico, the town was dedicated to Saint Francis. La Villa Real de la Santa Fe de San Francisco de Asis (The Royal City of the Holy Faith of Saint Francis of Assisi) was founded in 1609/10. Not only was Santa Fe dedicated to Saint Francis, but most of the settlers were dedicated to him as well. They were devoted members of the lay Third Order of Saint Francis. This Roman Catholic religious confraternity was meant to project brotherhood and spread goodwill. The Spanish military or presidio soldiers in Santa Fe and throughout the territory of New Mexico were also members. They were sworn to protect the Indians, and when they courageously gave up their lives, the soldiers were buried in the habit and cord of Saint Francis with the adobe brick. It is generally believed that all of the mystical saints in the ancient Catholic Church were buried in this fashion. The placing of

Bola de Lumbre. Ancient Spanish folklore claimed witches could transform into balls of fire and reach out at night. *Photo by Lucia Dolores de Aragón.*

the brick next to the feet was a transcendental tradition. They believed our direct communion with God eternally saves us for life after death.

In New Mexico, the dead were dead but not gone. The word *difunto* or *difunta* was used before each name for those who had passed on. There is no actual translation for this term—suffice it to say that it was a special word of endearment for the deceased, those who had died, but were still among us in spirit. It was a beautiful part of the history and culture of New Mexico. It was a perpetual link between this world and the supernatural.

What can we say about the supernatural? What can be believed, or not believed? Perhaps ancient stories about the supernatural in New Mexico reveal the truth. Believe it or not! Nadie le tiene mas miedo a lo extraño que los que no lo creen. No one is more afraid of the strange than those who don't believe. La muerte no solamente mira por las paginas de los libros de los ancianos. Death doesn't just look through pages of the books of the old!

NEW MEXICO'S INNER SUPERSTITIONS

Now are thoughts thou shalt not banish,
Now are visions ne'er to vanish;
From thy spirit shall they pass No more—
Like dew drops from the grass.
—Edgar Allan Poe

There is a heritage in Spanish New Mexico of myths, legends and history emanating from the dreaded black plagues in Europe. Paranoia existed in Europe about death and dying during these trying ages. Many popular present-day superstitions, myths and legends evolved from the plague epidemics. It is natural that early Spanish colonists brought these convictions and introduced them into New Mexico territory during the seventeenth century. Spanish folk artists in New Mexico produced a variety of death images. Some were simple death figures representing the Angel of Death. Others were more intricate death carts with a skeleton holding a bow and arrow or hatchets, meant to signify that death was reaching out to the living, so one had better be prepared. As usual, scholars are uncertain when these images first appeared in New Mexico. Superstitions have existed since the very founding of New Mexico.

Some of the superstitions we have today are now taken for granted:

Spanish brides in New Mexico had to wear veils at the wedding ceremony. If they did not, then they could be subject to Evil Eye.

Why is it that when someone sneezes you say, "God bless you?" It was believed that if this was not said a piece of the person's soul could be hopelessly released and lost.

The words *rest in peace*, or *RIP*, were chiseled into tombstones because it was believed those who did not rest in peace after death roamed as spirits.

The phrase "knock on wood" came from people knocking on coffins to listen and confirm the person was indeed dead. Premature burial was prevalent in history. This was frightening, especially when those buried woke up to find themselves deep underground in coffins. When it was finally realized this was happening, someone would knock on the wood coffin to see if there was a response before covering the coffin with dirt in the ground. Sometimes someone would knock back. In "The Premature Burial," Edgar Allan Poe states, "The boundaries which divide Life from Death are shadowy and vague. Who shall say where one ends, and where the other begins?"

Garlic around your neck keeps vampires and evil spirits away. Never leave your hair, eyelashes or nail parings lying around. A witch can get these and use them to cast an evil spell on you.

"Tonight upon your pillow, close your eyes and hide your head, for the witches and goblins will be hovering round your bed."

Do not put two mirrors in front of each other, because this will provide a threshold for spirits to enter your house.

A puzzling New Mexico riddle: "Touch your toes, touch your nose, never go in one of those, unless you see a spirit rose." What is it? The answer: a hearse.

If you spill salt, throw some over your shoulder or else you will have bad luck brought up by evil spirits standing behind you. The salt will blind them and keep them from harming you.

A New Mexico Spanish folk saying is "La muerte seca todas tus lagrimas."
(Death dries all your tears.) A poem by Victor Hugo, "The Grandmother,"
in the June 6, 1846 issue of the *Anglo American* follows in the same vein:

> *Ah! When thou shalt wake and find us, near the lamp that's ceased to burn,*
> *Dead, and when thou speakest to us, deaf and silent in our turn—*
> *Then, how great will be your sorrow! Then you'll cry for us in vain:*
> *Call upon your saint and patron for a long, long time and fain,*
> *And a long, long time embrace us, ere we come to life again!*

PATAS CHUECAS
(CROOKED FEET)

"I suppose you are going to tell me how this spirit is going to come to me at night and pull at my feet so that I will believe." Elena often heard from her nana how when she died she was going to come to her and pull at her feet until she would finally believe in the spirits of the dead. Elena did not believe but somehow she could not sleep at night if her feet were uncovered. It didn't matter how hot it was outside. "I don't think it is the dead we have to worry about," Elena responded. "I'm more afraid of the living." "We will see," her nana said.
—*Rosa Maria Calles,* Tale of the Wailing Woman

There is a very old story told around different parts of New Mexico about a man who was abusive, who shirked responsibilities to his family and who was a worthless ne'er-do-well. He was given different names. In one isolated New Mexico village called Ocate, he was known as Tomas Rendido, someone who had lived about the turn of the twentieth century—in 1905, to be exact. Rendido means one who "yielded" or "surrendered" himself. In Spanish, *pies* means "feet." Patas, Tomas's nickname, refers to the feet of an animal. They claim that when Tomas walked around the village of Ocate, the enormous sounds coming from his feet sounded pretty much like the loud clacking of a galloping horse that had no direction. That is why they called him *Patas Chuecas* (Crooked Feet).

Well, Patas really enjoyed having a good time. His favorite pastime was going to the local bar. It was called La Cantina de Salas, the Salas Bar. Salas comes from the word *salir*, meaning "to leave." In other words, leave if you can. Patas always found many friends there. They all brought him

New Mexico valley. Folklore and legends refer to many stories of supernatural sightings occurring at rivers, arroyos and hidden places.

drinks. Wine, whiskey, gin, rum, brandy and beer flowed freely at the Salas Bar. The drink that the good-for-nothing liked most though was *aguardiente*, which means "watered-down teeth." That was indeed strange. Whose teeth? His wife, María Cristina, was known as La Chiqueona—in New Mexico regional Spanish, "one who complains about everything." I'm sure you've heard the old song "María Cristina Me Quiere Gobernar" (María Cristina Wants to Control Me). That song was about her. It is quite understandable why María Cristina would complain. She worked her fingers to the bone while her worthless husband did nothing more than take it easy and relax every single day. He really liked to chill as they say now. She had to take care of their many children, cook and clean.

Rock house in New Mexico territory, which was a vast southwestern area. Spirit-filled dwellings are favorites with ghost hunters. Note camera tripod by door.

Anyway, one very dark and foreboding day, Patas stealthily snuck out of the house. He joyously but carefully made his way to the bar while looking over his shoulders for his wife. She was nowhere to be seen. Patas really wanted to celebrate his good fortune of finding such a hardworking wife. He thanked God and all of the santos every day. She complained, as she always did, but for some fantastic reason, she put up with him and loved him. As they say in New Mexico, "Nunca falta una rota para un descocido." Misery loves company.

On this particularly black night, Patas had an especially good time. He and his compadres performed somber and passionate rituals with one toast after another as they drank heavily. They sang happy and tear-filled Spanish songs that were as old as the sky is blue, such as "Cielito Lindo" (Beautiful Sky), to extoll the beauty of a fabulous girl. They also sang "El Rancho Grande," which praises a big ranch and cowboys, and "De Colores," a nice song about the pleasantness of life in New Mexico in general.

Then one very special señorita caught the droopy eyes of Patas. She sat all by herself in a far corner of the bar. She was partially obscured by the darkness. She was staring at him with beautiful eyes through dark lashes. Her long flowing black hair almost reached the floor. Interestingly, when Patas searched to look at her smooth face with its creamy complexion, she would wink and then turn away. The mysterious young woman would place her delightful hand on the side of her lovely face. She had the most beautiful long fingers with an alluring polish. He had never seen anything like that in his entire life. One couldn't even begin to describe her hands. They glowed in the faint light.

After partying for endless hours, Patas called it a night. A full mystical moon lit his path home. Patas was filled with thoughts about what a great time he had just had on this bright night. Better than any other night. His enormous feet clicked and clapped on the way home. Suddenly, his night exceeded those nights from before. There was a movement, a fleeting glimpse, and then the young woman from the bar stood right in front of him. Once again, she winked and said, "Hello Tomas, how is it going?" How could it be that this ravishing beauty knew his name? However, Tomas was indeed perplexed. Patas thought he had died and had gone to heaven. He started to think she had seen him before and actually liked him.

A pasted smile on Patas's droopy face began to grow. It got steadily wider. You wouldn't believe what then happened. The radiant woman slowly, then quickly, turned old and wrinkled. She was death personified. This dark creature let out a hideous shriek, and then poor Patas heard her piercing cry. That heart-wrenching wail traveled everywhere. You couldn't escape it. It touched your soul and your very being. The panicked drunk took off

Ven a Mi (*Come to Me*). Painting by Rosalinda Pacheco. At times, inviting spirits drew the living to go with them.

La Llorona. The famous Wailing Woman appears from hiding to draw an innocent victim to death. *Photo of Rosalía de Aragón as the spirit by Rosa María Calles.*

like an arrow. Death followed him and reached out, touching his flinching shoulders. Patas desperately tried to get away. He could feel her cold and clammy hands. His pounding feet made such loud noises that they woke up the entire sleepy village of Ocate.

Patas finally made it to his home. He banged as hard as he could on the door. María Cristina woke up from a beautiful dream. She was in heaven on the clouds, singing along with the pretty angels who were playing their harps. Then reality struck her. She had to open the door. Thankfully, the children were still asleep in their rooms. Her husband's face was as white as a sheet. Patas screamed for help and rushed in. "Someone is chasing me," he yelled. María Cristina looked outside but saw nothing except for an owl that glared at her and hooted. There were also sounds of wolves off in the distance and scampering coyotes nearby.

The disgruntled villagers say they learned that Patas went straight to the family altar with its lit candles. The saintly wooden statues seemed to move

The eternal spirit of La Llorona, New Mexico's most famous phantom, as portrayed by Rosalía de Aragón, is inviting. *Photo by Rosa María Calles.*

with the flickering of the flames. The sorrow-filled man was repentant. Patas was so sorry he had neglected his family. He always had excuses for not going to church. The santos at the altar cast shadows on the walls. The images of San Miguel, San Isidro and San José spoke to Patas. He prayed until the morning sun came up. There is a very old saying in Spanish, "No hay mal que por bien no venga." (There isn't anything bad that happens that something good will come out of it.) Patas was certain La Llorona appeared to him. She is that wailing spirit that travels about during the darkness of night. Her nightly crying appearance means different things to different people. Patas really did something good. He became a very devoted member of La Hermandad de Nuestro Padre Jesús Nazareno. This ancient group in New Mexico reenacts the Passion of Jesus Christ each Lent and is actively involved in the corporal works of mercy—that is, helping all of those who are desperately in need of help like he was.

Opposite: Finis Coronat. Latin for "The End Crowns the Work." *Jan Van der Deyster, Leyden, 1732. Public domain.*

Selected References

Barber, Paul. *Vampires, Burial and Death: Folklore and Reality*. New Haven, CT: Yale University Press, 1988.

Benavides, Alonso de. *Memorial of 1630*. Translated by Mrs. Edward E. Ayer. Albuquerque, NM: Horn and Wallace, 1965.

Bondeson, Jan. *Buried Alive: The Terrifying History of Our Most Primal Fear*. New York: W.W. Norton and Company, 2001.

Bower, Bruce. "Prehistoric Hand Axes Older Than Once Thought." *Science News*, September 3, 2009.

Brown, Lorin W. *Hispano Folklife of New Mexico*. Albuquerque: University of New Mexico Press, 1973.

Bryan, Howard. *Robbers, Rogues and Ruffians*. Santa Fe, NM: Clear Light Publishers, 1991.

Bullock, Alice. *Living Legends of Santa Fe Country*. Santa Fe, NM: Ancient City Press, 1972.

———. *Mountain Villages*. Santa Fe, NM: Sunstone Press, 1981.

Callon, Milton W. *Las Vegas, New Mexico: The Town that Wouldn't Gamble*. Las Vegas, NM: Las Vegas Daily Optic, 1962.

C. de Baca. *Legends of a Hermit*. Las Vegas, NM: private printing, n.d..

Charman, Neil. "The Enigma of Ball Lightning." *New Scientist* 56 (December 1972): 632–35.

Chavez, Tibo J. *New Mexican Folklore of the Rio Abajo*. Portales, NM: Bishop Publishing, 1972.

Clark, Ardy Sixkiller. *Encounters with the Star People: Untold Stories of American Indians*. San Antonio, TX: Anomalist Books, 2012.

Coca, Benjamin, PhD. *Del Pasado al Presente—From the Past to the Present: The Hermit and Other Histories*. Montezuma, NM: Montezuma Press, 1977.

Cordova, Lorenzo de. *Echoes of the Flute*. Santa Fe, NM: Ancient City Press, 1985.

Cruz, Joan Carroll. *Relics*. Huntington, IN: Our Sunday Visitor, 1984.

Darley, Alex M. *The Passionists of the Southwest*. Glorieta, NM: Rio Grande Press, 1968.

De Agreda, Maria. *Mystical City of God*. Translated by Marison Fiscar. Washington, D.C.: AMI Press, 1971.

De Aragón, Ray John. *Enchanted Legends and Lore of New Mexico: Witches, Ghosts, and Spirits*. Charleston, SC: The History Press, 2012.

———. *Haunted Santa Fe*. Charleston, SC: The History Press, 2018.

———. *The Legend of La Llorona*. Santa Fe, NM: Sunstone Press, 2006.

———. *New Mexico Book of the Undead: Goblin and Ghoul Folklore*. Charleston, SC: The History Press, 2014.

———. *The Penitentes of New Mexico*. Santa Fe, NM: Sunstone Press, 2006.

DeBorhegyi, Stephen H. *El Santuario de Chimayo*. Santa Fe, NM: Spanish Colonial Arts Society, 1956.

Dibble, Christopher. "The Dead Ringer: Medicine, Poe, and the Fear of Premature Burial." *Historia Medicinæ* 2, no. 1 (2010). https://sites.google.com/a/medicinae.org/historia-medicinae/e16.

Dundes, Alan. *The Evil Eye: A Casebook*. Madison: University of Wisconsin Press, 1992.

Edwards, Richard, and Hopewell M. Edwards. *Edward's Great West*. St. Louis: Edward's Monthly, 1860.

Egan, Martha. *Milagros, Votive Offerings from the Americas*. Santa Fe: Museum of New Mexico Press, 1991.

Gamache, Henri. *Terrors of the Evil Eye Exposed*. New York: Raymond Publishing, 1946.

Garcia, Nasario. *Tales of Witchcraft and the Supernatural in the Pecos Valley*. Santa Fe, NM: Western Edge Press, 1999.

Good, Timothy. *Need to Know: UFOs, the Military and Intelligence*. New York: Pegasus Books, 2007.

Gordon, Richard. *The Alarming History of Medicine*. New York: St. Martin's Press, 1994.

Gottfried, Robert S. *The Black Death*. New York: Macmillan, 1983.

Hibben, Frank C. *Treasure in the Dust: Archaeology in the New World*. London: Claver-Hume Press, Ltd., 1953.

Hickerson, Nancy Parrott. *The Jumanos: Hunters and Traders of the South Plains*. Austin: University of Texas Press, 1994.

Kendrick, T.D. *Mary of Agreda: The Life and Legend of a Spanish Nun*. New York: Routledge & Kegan Paul, 1967.

Kessell, John L. *Kiva, Cross, and Crown: The Pecos Indians and New Mexico 1540–1840*. Albuquerque: University of New Mexico Press, 1979.

Lopez-Gaston, Jose R. *Tradicion Hispanica de Nuevo Mexico: Hispanic Traditions of New Mexico*. Mexico: Editorial Progreso, S.A., 1985.

Marison, Fiscar, Translator. *City of God: The Transfixion*. Washington, D.C.: AMI Press, 1988.

Meleski, Patricia. *Echoes of the Past*. Albuquerque: University of New Mexico Press, 1972.

Moore, Michael. *Medicinal Plants of the Mountain West*. Santa Fe: Museum of New Mexico Press, 1979.

Myer, Felicia A. *Traditional Herbs of New Mexico*. Albuquerque, NM: Rio Grande Herb, 1994.

New York Times. "Balls of Fire Stalk U.S. Fighters in Night Assaults Over Germany." January 2, 1945.

Nobel, David, Grant. *In Search of Chaco: New approaches to an Archaeological Enigma*. Santa Fe, NM: School of American Research, 2004.

Painter, Sidney. *A History of the Middle Ages*. New York: Knopf, 1956.

Panofsky, Erwin. *Studies in Iconology*. New York: Harper and Rowe, 1972.

Perrigo, Lynn Irwin. *Gateway to Glorieta: A History of Las Vegas, New Mexico*. Santa Fe, NM: Sunstone Press, 2010.

Sheehan, Michael J., ed. *Four Hundred Years of Faith: A History of the Catholic Church in New Mexico*. Albuquerque, NM: Archdiocese of Santa Fe, 1998.

Sons of the Holy Family. *El Santuario: A Stop on the High Road to Taos*. Silver Spring, MD: Sons of the Holy Family, 1994.

Tate, Bill. *The Penitentes of the Sangre de Cristos*. Truchas, NM: Tate Gallery, 1968.

Toor, Frances. *A Treasury of Mexican Folkways*. New York: Crown, 1947.

Twitchell, Ralph Emerson. *Leading Facts of New Mexican History*. Santa Fe: Sunstone Press, 2007.

Ulibarri, Sabine R. *Primeros Encuentros, First Encounters*. Ypsilanti, MI: Bilingual Press, 1982.

Weigle, Marta. *Brothers of Light, Brothers of Blood*. Albuquerque: University of New Mexico Press, 1976.

ABOUT THE AUTHOR

R ay John de Aragón received his master's degree in American Studies from New Mexico Highlands University on May 10, 1986. He concentrated on the Spanish colonial arts and ethnohistory of New Mexico and was inducted into the Honor Society of Phi Kappa Phi. De Aragón's anthropological studies included cultural traditions, heritage and paranormal superstitions of the people. The author has lectured and presented often about his fascinating discoveries concerning New Mexico supernatural phenomena, influences and lore. He found that beliefs in spirits and unexplained paranormal appearances and contacts are prevalent in ancient and recent New Mexico myths and legends. Ray John has investigated and explored various mysteries of the past not only as an amateur archaeologist but also as one seeking answers to age-old questions. He received a literary award from former Albuquerque mayor Harry Kinney on August 27, 1983; a first-place traditional arts award from Mayor Martin Chavez presented on April 28, 1995; and the Quality Education Award in Arts by the New Mexico Research and Study Council of the University of New Mexico in 2007.